CATHOLICISM REVISITED

Inigo Text Series: 11

CATHOLICISM REVISITED

On Re-imagining God

Robert Butterworth

GRACEWING

First published in 2007

Gracewing
2 Southern Avenue,
Leominster
Herefordshire HR6 0QF

Inigo Enterprises
Links View
Traps Lane, New Malden
Surrey KT3 4RY

*'The expense is reckoned; the enterprise is begun
It is of God ...'*

All rights reserved. No part of this publication may be reproduced, stored in a retrieval system, or transmitted in any form, or by any means, electronic, mechanical, photocopying, recording, or otherwise, without the written permission of the publisher.

© Robert Butterworth 2007

The right of Robert Butterworth to be identified as the author of this work has been asserted in accordance with the Copyright, Designs and Patents Act 1988.

ISBN 978-0-85244-142-8

Cover image: Detail from *Christ Before Pilate* by Matthias Stom, c. 1635. Reproduced by kind permission of Campion Hall, Oxford.

Typesetting by
Action Publishing Technology Ltd, Gloucester GL1 5SR

Contents

Foreword		vii
Introduction		xi
1.	**Prolegomena**	1
2.	**Faith**	63
3.	**Theologoumena**	95
4.	**Salvation**	126
5.	**Church**	171
6.	**Conclusion**	193

Foreword

Imagining and re-imagining – and not least in religion – is a more important process than is commonly allowed. George Bernard Shaw realized this in his soldiers' reaction to Joan of Arc: 'You're just imagining these visions' – meaning, 'Come out of your world of fantasy and unreality' – and Joan replied: 'Of course, I'm imagining it – that's how God speaks to me'. Retired from the professional religious life and from lecturing in theology at university, Robert Butterworth remained determined to discover how his Catholicism was meant to work and to produce its saving spiritual effects; and this led him to examine the necessary function of the theological imagination in coming to terms with our experience of our own mystery-bound humanity which, he claims, is the very basis of a mature Catholicism.

He is in a good position to do this, writing as he does with the precision of a classicist and the imaginative feeling of a romanticist. His book grew naturally out of his more autobiographical *The Detour – Towards Revising Catholicism* (Gracewing, 2005), with its attractive evocation of a Lancashire Catholic childhood in the 1930s and 1940s, and his tale of the forty years he spent in the Jesuits; but it develops the final chapter of that book into a searching and passionate exposition of his personal understanding and interpretation of his native Catholicism. He calls on several scholarly disciplines – philological, philosophical, theological, literary – for their contributions, and he gives what he discerns as the mystical and visionary nature of Catholic faith an unusual and striking prominence. This nature he carefully explores in the light both of the human faith of the Jesus who originally inspired the Catholic vision, and of the theological interpretation which St Paul was first to give it. Since he is by training a dogmatic theologian, especially familiar with the early history of the Catholic doctrinal tradition, it is not surprising that the function and meaning of the Catholic system of beliefs comes in for some serious rethinking which, however, leaves the system perhaps even more essential to Catholic faith than it has tended to become. The doctrines of the Incarnation and of the Trinity emerge as absolutely central to his Catholicism and definitive of the way in which he thinks Catholics must re-imagine their God.

But his book is by no means a nostalgic revisiting and reassertion of the Catholic values of some 'Brideshead' past. He is intensely convinced of Catholicism's need for a radically revised future. In fact, despite adopting the relaxed form and tone of an essay, he displays a notably radical intensity throughout. He pulls no punches and cuts no corners. Loyal as he remains to the Catholic tradtion, he gives a clear impression that much honest soul searching and sustained intelligent reflection has gone into his work. His criticism of the institutional Church is trenchant but balanced. He gives vivid and honest treatment to the problems raised for faith and belief by history and philosophy and by the universal factor of interpretation through metaphor and imagination. His chief focus is on the humanity of Jesus as the main source of any valid Catholic theology. If at times he seems to understress divinity, this is because he has both re-imagined divinity on the non-theistic and radically human lines which he sees as demanded by the doctrine of the Incarnation, and at the same time he has been determined to bring out the real importance of the transformative doctrine of the Trinity. Above all, he is not afraid of speaking in terms of religious mystery and vision as the human, existential springs from which Catholicism draws its characteristic promise of salvation.

Yet for all this, he sees that such profundities are meant simply to help us realize that Catholicism presents the living of a truly human life under grace as a very ordinary daily process consistently inspired by the human faith, hope and love discernible in the life and death and resurrection of Jesus. Defined by the mystery of his own humanity as revealed in Jesus, and led by a vision of reality which is articulated by his beliefs, the Catholic is encouraged to live a personal and social life which from day to day brings out the fullness of the glory of being human. In this way his findings belong firmly to the mainstream of Catholic spirituality.

This is a very personal testament by Robert Butterworth to his Catholic faith. My commendation does not imply that I personally or the Society of Jesus are in agreement with all of his proposals. Professional theologians will be able to make more informed comments than I can. However, this book does provide an articulate and original discussion of important questions that I am sure many Catholics as well as many others will find enlightening and helpful. It serves as a model in method and content for anyone who wants to appreciate more personally and more fully the abiding reality of Jesus Christ.

Fr Billy Hewett, SJ
Campion Hall
Oxford

Introduction

I should make it clear from the start that the book I have written is an extended personal essay which shares the limitations, but makes the most of the advantages, of that particular genre. It is an attempt to suggest how Catholicism, too often viewed simply as a religious system administered by a Church, needs to be seen as a way of spiritual salvation at the hands of a God, the understanding of whose uniquely characteristic mystery must constantly invite fresh efforts of the human mind and imagination. In brief, I think the time has come for the Catholic God to be re-imagined.

By spiritual salvation I do not mean anything airy-fairy or alien or exotic, but a practical, relevant, quotidian, down-to-earth way of coping seriously with the mystery of being human, and of making the best and the most of it. What I want to know is how Catholicism is meant to work spiritually as a way of salvation for its adherents: that is, as a way of bringing about, in the unique spirit of the man whose religious insights are the inspiration of Catholicism, the amendment, enhancement and fulfilment of humankind's obviously flawed potential. I base my remarks on a lifetime's experience of Roman Catholicism which included forty years of unregretted intimacy with its institutional reality as a Jesuit, with over half of those years spent teaching academic theology. This experience seems to me to amount to a sufficiently valid set of qualifications for trying to undertake the sort of enquiry I have in mind; though it remains to be seen how acceptable my conclusions turn out to be. I have also drawn on certain long-standing problems I have had with the way official Catholicism presents itself as a religious system, on some acquired theological learning, and, more deeply, on a measure of imaginative interpretation. My sole purpose is to try and see if Catholicism can be made more credible by an elucidation of its spiritual workings.

I think it is right to explain that my approach and my conclusions derive from a long tussle I have had with myself. Apart from the personal factors inevitably involved in it – I have dealt with these elsewhere, and they need not concern others in the present context – I find it helpful to view the tussle as a progressive and creative confrontation between two different mentalities. I would label these mentalities 'classicism' and 'romanticism'. In my case, for one reason or another, an early sowing of the classicist mentality has somehow led, over the years, to the late flowering of romanticist attitudes. I was privileged to undergo a very long and thorough training in both classics and theology, rigorously conducted on classicist lines. This meant that I learned, among many other things, the supreme importance of the authority of established institutions, of approved writers, of standard views, of model texts, and of the scrupulous but formally dead tradition of words themselves in the processes of learning – processes whose validity rested on the applicability of public and rational criteria above all other considerations. Personal interests or enthusiasms, where they emerged, were there to be contained or suppressed. Truth was to be acquired with certainty through closely attending to the logic of systematic learning, and there was the end of the affair. This is a wonderful legacy to inherit, and I remain deeply grateful for it.

But when the time eventually came to turn to a deeper, more seriously personal consideration of my own Catholicism I found that the classical approach fell far short of penetrating to what I had slowly come to consider the heart of the matter. To discover what that heart consisted in seemed to call for a distinctly different approach. So gradually I was led to adopt what I have labelled a more romanticist approach towards Catholicism. Romanticism, in this context, has nothing to do with sentimentality, though it involves the feelings. It indicates a mode of cognition, of knowledge, which makes much more allowance for personal factors than does classicism. It suits Catholicism, so it seems to me, better than classicism. After all, as a religion, Catholicism is inevitably an affair of the heart as well as of the mind, and – even more importantly, as I hope to show – it is an affair of felt experience and the creative imagination. So I wish to recruit my own long, personal experience of it, along with my growing sense of the basic and essential mysticism of Catholicism (I think 'mysticism' is the only word for it), into my attempt to understand it better. Why should such valued factors be discounted? Why should the individual imagination, as well as the reason, not be brought into creative play in understanding and interpreting Catholicism, in searching it out, not just as a coherent and efficient religious system, but as an effective path to spiritual salvation? After all, was it not meant to be understood spiritually? I felt encouraged by Catholicism itself to move into a romanticist mode of understanding its spirituality; and I am led to reflect that it may be that it is exclusively classicist attempts to account for a predominantly romanticist phenomenon like Catholicism (and no doubt other religions) which generate precisely the kind of intractable problems with which we commonly find such religions beset.

I consider that the shift from a classicist to a romanticist approach is one of the reasons why I have been led to put such emphasis in this book on the use and meaning of words. As I see it, one sound way of distinguishing between the two approaches is to note not only the different ways in which they use words and names but also the difference in what meaning and understanding and truth amount to in both approaches. The way a classicist uses words has about it an air of confident finality, of essential definition, of the solution of a problem. It is as if reason comes to rest with the imposition of a word or name which spells the end of the matter, at least for the time being, or until the problem reappears and a new but similar solution has to be worked out. A romanticist proceeds quite differently. Here a word or name is creatively discovered by the imagination and is used, not to stifle further inquiry, but to reveal, as best it can for the moment, what can only be called the existential or living mystery of the thing in question. Here a word is a response to the standing invitation extended by such mystery. If a classicist approach tends towards closure, and towards the acquisition of the certainty it always seems to need, a romanticist approach leads to openness, to a broad tolerance, to the promise of fresh starts, to an inward certainty of a different kind, and towards facing, and forging, the world with new interpretations and understandings.

I am attracted to the theological conceit which supposes that the biblical God of creation was inclined to the classicist approach. He created and gave definitive shape to his new world and its contents by the use of words and names: 'And God said ... And it was so' (Genesis 1:9). Adam, his human creature, picked up the classicist habit from his creator:

> 'So out of the ground the LORD God formed every animal of the field and every bird of the air, and brought them to the man to see what he would call them; and whatever the man called each living creature, that was its name. The man gave names to all the cattle, and to the birds of the air, and to every animal of the field ... (Genesis 2:19–20)

But the God of Catholic salvation is much more openly a romanticist in his approach. His Word, divine and actively creative as it continues to be, operates in a wholly new mode. This Word is now alive with his own basic humanity, and in such a thorough way as to make him both the enlightenment and salvation of humankind and also wholly vulnerable to all the vagaries of human life – to being ignored and rejected and eventually killed, as well as to being recognized and welcomed and – astonishingly – victorious over death. It is in and through his very humanity that this Word bespeaks openness, mystery, imaginative understanding, the radical reinterpretation of established religious tradition, striking novelty, tolerance, forgiveness, resurrection, and, above all, a salvation that consists in constant beginnings and renewals – 'In the *beginning* was the Word ...' (John 1:1).

Accordingly, over the years I underwent a thorough *metanoia* – a basic shift of mind-set. My approach to Catholicism has become gradually more romanticist and more human, and so more centred on the imaginative use of words and names. By this I mean that, picking up the masterly theological hints contained in the fundamental Catholic doctrine of the Incarnation (the divine Word made man), I have found it best to try to understand Catholicism from the point of view of our common humanity as a form of deeply human spirituality or – as I shall go so far as to suggest – a mysticism which leads us directly to God in the depths of our own humanity. My approach is 'from below', rather than 'from above'. If the classicist's God and his promised Beyond do not seem to figure as much as they might be expected to in my account of Catholicism, this is because I think the character of Catholicism renders them passé; and loose talk about such a God and such a Beyond runs the risk of missing what I consider to be the unique truth which a fuller, truer understanding of Catholicism has to offer. So much of our habitual talk about God and the Beyond contrives to be not only uncritically obscure, it also ignores that particular sense of our common human mystery without which Catholicism, in my view, cannot be expected to make sense and to work spiritually. I maintain that the mystery at the heart of existing as a human being – that is, as this individual human person and as no one else – is far from being a matter of mere obscurity, and even further from being a source of theological problems or puzzles or conundrums. It amounts to the very mystery which Catholics need to mean by God. Such a mystery needs to be allowed to shed its own light; whereas classicist theology, not least when poorly understood and unthinkingly pursued, simply serves to thicken the darkness. Hence I make much of what I discern as the real mystery inherent in being human itself, a mystery so luminously close to us that we habitually fail to notice it – the sheer fact that each person happens to exist as what and who they precisely are. This emphasis is licensed, I think, by taking seriously both the experience of being human and the fundamental Catholic doctrine of the Incarnation.

The fact is that I have not been able to make sense of the spirituality of Catholicism without having to re-imagine what I mean by God. This is a bold move to make, but given the claims of Catholicism, it ought not to be surprising. Both the distinctiveness and the universality of Catholicism seem to me ultimately to require it. I have had to try to re-imagine God because I have had to try to re-imagine – in my own clumsy way – what it is like to be human. Given the intensity of the way in which God and humankind are believed to relate to one another in orthodox Catholicism, it would be wrong not to expect such radical alterations to the way we are meant to think of both.

Perhaps a final word is called for regarding the style and tone of what I have written. I have not wanted to involve readers in all the running discussions and arguments I have had with myself over the years; nor have I detailed the reading and research that lie behind many of my conclusions. I did not want to write that sort of book, but a lighter, handier, more relaxed essay which would allow me to enjoy the kind of informality which better suits the often tentative nature of what I want to say – and which might challenge readers who are interested in asking my kind of questions about Catholicism to go away and do better; or if they disagree with me, to try and work out their own answers. The book I have written is, of course, idiosyncratic: it consists of personal conclusions which have accumulated from various sources over a long time. I suspect they are far from incorrigible. If they are found to be dry and to lack practical application, this is because I consider it a priority to try to clarify the inner structure and spiritual workings of Catholicism rather than to preach it or to illustrate it with examples. In the end, there is nothing more practical than getting the understanding of something right. If there has been significant distortion in the way Catholicism has been presented, then considerable readjustment will be required to reclaim and reveal its working shape. There is no way of making such a readjustment without bringing up technical, and especially linguistic, issues. My conclusions mark such progress as I think I have managed to make so far in understanding what I hold to be the saving truth of Catholicism.

Scriptural quotations, except where I have thought it best to translate them myself, whether in the interests of clarity or of a permissibly broader interpretation, are from the New Revised Standard Version (NRSV) of the Bible (Anglicized Edition), Oxford University Press, 1998.

For conciliar texts in the original languages I have used the ever-handy *Enchiridion Symbolorum, Definitionum et Declarationum de Rebus Fidei et Morum*, originally edited by Heinrich Denzinger and thoroughly revised by Adolf Schönmetzer SJ, 34th edition, Freiburg im Breisgau, 1965. My translations of these are referred to as Denzinger-Schönmetzer.

It remains for me to thank Fr Clarence Gallagher and especially Fr Billy Hewett, both of the Society of Jesus, for the consistent practical help which was essential for the production of this book. I would like it to be noted that the ideas and views I have expressed are those of the author – they are not necessarily those of Inigo Enterprises or of anyone in the Society of Jesus. What I have written inevitably owes most to my wife, Barbara, who is the best Catholic I know. The publishers and myself are grateful to Campion Hall, Oxford, for permission to print the reproduction of Matthias Stom's *Christ Before Pilate*.

R. B.
Cowley, Uxbridge

Chapter 1

Prolegomena

> The prologues are over. It is a question, now,
> Of final belief. So, say that final belief
> Must be in a fiction. It is time to choose.
>
> Wallace Stevens, *Asides on the Oboe*

It is some years ago now that these challenging lines first caught my attention and began occasionally to haunt me. My life, like anyone else's, has passed through several phases, each of which might be construed as some kind of prologue to the phase that followed it. Up to now it has all amounted to a far from unhappy experience of being alive. If happiness consists in realizing how lucky you are – and I suspect it mainly does – then I have been a generally happy person. But I am also getting older, and I realize that the phases, the prologues still to come, if there are any, must be few in number. So the notion of achieving a state of 'final belief', as I have chosen to understand it, becomes attractive. I take 'final' to mean, not some set of conclusions declared definitively valid and certain, but, in a broader sense, a decent measure of closure to the kind of religious questionings, personal as well as professional, that have accompanied me through so much of life – a general settling of those issues regarding the meaning of my Catholic beliefs which have long exercised me.

But the disturbing, even shocking, sting in Stevens's lines is that I might find myself looking at 'a fiction'. I think I know roughly how much the expression meant to him, given his intriguing views on the nature and function of poetry; and I have – as I hope to show – considerable sympathy with the notion that the fictive constructs of the imagination and the invention of metaphors play an indispensable role in the way we can know and live with the things of this world. But as a bald account of what religious beliefs might amount to, 'a fiction' will hardly do. Whilst there can be no doubt that it has its own way of telling the truth, fiction, vulgarly opposed to fact, is nowadays too much identified with untruth and falsehood. At root its verb (*fingere*) denotes a hands-on, 'plastic' activity: it is a word for forming, moulding, shaping, fashioning, making things – at first with the hands, and eventually with the mind and the imagination: inventing, supposing, devising, representing, constructing, creating ideas. Its decline into feigning, deceiving, lying is all too easy to foresee. Still, the process of framing fictions of various kinds – myths, fables and so forth – has long served as a way of coping with a complex and difficult world; and we still need to make rational hypotheses, reasoned suppositions, so that understanding can proceed – to put certain fictive constructions on our world in order to make it tolerably comfortable and to live intelligently in it. The process of fiction is clearly not confined to the arts. Serious science has recourse to it. It appears to be the case, for instance, that certain modern cosmological concepts are products of fiction. Examples might be 'dark matter' and 'dark energy', neither of which has proved – as I understand it – to be empirically detectable so far, but which are conceptually required to make sense of the latest view of the universe and its origins. The process of their formulation calls for and employs the conscious use of fiction.

But if the *process* of their formulation is properly called fiction, I hardly think that a scientist whose world-view depends on them would be inclined to dismiss them as 'a fiction', or even as merely fictional. Much the same seems to me to be true of religious beliefs. They are found by many to be necessary in order to make sense of the world in which they have to live. There can be no doubt that theologians have had to employ fiction of a sophisticated, even colourful, kind in the *process* of formulating those beliefs. But to relegate them comprehensively to being 'a fiction', and to dismiss them because they have been arrived at by the only process open to their formulation would, it seems to me, be an unintelligent reaction.

Prolegomena

Fictions, like myths and fables, tell truths about our world – truths that cannot be told as well, or perhaps at all, in other ways. Think, say, of the Catholic belief in creation. The whole process of its formulation, from the Bible onwards, draws on the use of theological fiction. But as a formulated belief it plays a highly effective, and even indispensable, part in the whole orientation of the Catholic faith-vision of the world. It would seem to me quite as misguided for a believer to dismiss the belief in creation as 'a fiction' or as 'fictional', as it would be for a modern scientist to dismiss 'dark matter', just because its formulation as a concept has necessarily involved the process of fiction. Both religion and science find themselves dealing with matters beyond empirical verification in order to make sense of their different worlds: permanently beyond, in the case of religion, temporarily beyond, in the case of science – until, that is, some appropriate method of verification is discovered, or an alternative scientific fiction is proposed. Despite all this I feel it is wise to avoid the word 'fiction', and perhaps even 'fictional', in my search for a better, spiritual understanding of Catholicism, if only because they might appear to rule out truth.

I have always been a Roman Catholic, and I still am. I cannot imagine myself belonging to any other persuasion. Much of my academic career was spent researching and teaching the history of Christian beliefs, not least the formative beliefs of the early Christian centuries. From my studies there arose, from time to time, unsurprising problems regarding the interpretation and understanding of those beliefs. I still want to be able to count them as beliefs which have their contribution – whatever it is – to make towards the expression of religious truth; but before I can do that, I shall need to know in what sense I am supposed to take them. Without knowing what my beliefs are meant to mean – what use they are, how they are meant to work – I cannot begin to say in what sense they are true. What study and experience have done is to render me incapable of approaching my beliefs, as it were, the other way round. I can no longer simply accept their truth – and least of all on someone else's say-so – and then on that basis assume that their meaningfulness and what they actually mean need no further examination. But are they – can they possibly be? – what they appear to describe: a God-revealed account of activities and states of affairs that belong to some literal Beyond? Or do they refer, in some roundabout way, to some deeper dimension of the Here and Now? It seems worthwhile trying to find out, if only in the hope of achieving that state of 'final belief', in which, some dramatic death-bed conversion apart, I feel I can happily end my days.

※

Such is the background and the life-setting, the *Sitz im Leben*, of this book. It was never going to be easy to write. The project of discovering what my Catholic beliefs are meant to mean, what religious use they are, how they are meant to work, led me to see that there was no chance of answering such questions without an all-round look at Catholicism as a religion. No good whatever could come, it seems to me, from just scrutinizing my Catholic beliefs as abstract and isolated specimens of religious speech-acts in the sterile conditions of a philosopher's study. They would need to be understood organically, in terms of their embedded function within Catholicism, to see where they fitted; and more importantly, in terms of how they actually worked as a prominent and active feature in the religion of Catholicism. So I could see that I was going to have to consider Catholicism as a whole; to strip down Catholicism as I saw it into its constituent elements and working parts, to see the origin and nature and use of Catholic beliefs – to see what they are *for* – and so to come to understand what meaning they were meant to have. The danger, of course, of probing into any living system is that, unless you are a very skilful operator, you will kill it – or, just as when you dismantle any working unit, you might never be able to put it all back together again; or you might put it back together again in a shape different from the shape in which you found it; or, as tends to happen, you might have some bits left over which now do not seem to fit anywhere and were possibly redundant or

Prolegomena 5

just decorative in the first place. Would anything like this happen if I began to take my Catholicism apart? Well, I was prepared to risk it, if only because my personal views are hardly likely to damage or alter Catholicism's official perception of itself; and because in any case I have no intention of trying to undermine so durable a construction. I just wanted to see if I could work out for myself that desirable state of 'final belief'.

I am aware, of course, that all this will sound the height of arrogance to some. They will say: Who do you think you are? Why bother your head about such matters? Why not let the Church and the tried-and-tested Catholic system take care of them? But nowadays I am much less prepared than I was to abandon my own personal responsibility for the way I decide to understand my own religious beliefs. After all, the way I find I can come to terms with them has a direct bearing on whatever effectiveness they are supposed to have within the personal salvation Catholicism claims it has to offer me. I do not feel pleased or proud of fetching up in this position at my time of life. I am certainly not proposing myself as an example to others. If I happen to have problems with what Catholic beliefs actually mean, and with how they are meant to work, I am aware that millions of good – far better – Catholics do not share those problems. At Sunday morning Mass in our local parish I like to look round with interest at what is going on. It is a decent, well-run parish, and Mass is celebrated in a straightforward, unfussy, devoutly down-to-earth fashion. The clergy are anything but flashy or trendy, and the sermons are sound and not unhelpful. The congregation is an ethnic mix, with many Irish and even more Asians and Afro-Caribbean faithful. I do not for a moment doubt that their Catholic beliefs, sincerely held, have always meant a great deal to them; and that those beliefs are religiously effective for them. They strike me as intelligent people, too. The Catholics I see around me at Mass know well what is going on; they know why they are there and how it is meant to affect them. I might even find it in myself to envy them, and to regret that I cannot share their unquestioning hold on their Catholic beliefs, though I still share their Catholic faith.

The fact is that, perhaps surprisingly, I do not find that having my kind of problem with the meaning and use of my Catholic *beliefs* immediately brings what I understand as my Catholic *faith* into question. If I happen to have lighted on a real problem with my Catholic beliefs, I would say that, given my privileged and specialized academic and religious background, I have a duty as a Catholic to try to sort it out, at least for myself. I know former Catholics who claim that their Catholicism, whether intellectually or in practice, has become too problematic and burdensome, and has thereby ceased to support them in their lives or make any contribution to their personal well-being. For them their Catholic religion, as well as their allegiance to the Church whose responsibility it is to preserve and promote it, now lies in their personal past. I can quite understand their position, and I do not doubt their sincerity. It is not for me to speculate why some people choose to drop out of Catholicism: it is simply that I find I have no reason or wish to drop out of it myself. Any kind of believing is a personally complex business. A. E. Housman once sourly remarked: 'Mankind believes things not because it has reasons for believing them, but because it has motives, and abandons beliefs not because they are incredible but because they are uncongenial.' But if this is meant to be true of believing in general, it may be thought to fall well short of describing the complexity of religious believing, which seems to me to be best treated as a distinct and unique instance of believing, and as one that is likely to generate real problems which arise not only from the intrusion of subjective attitudes, but also from the peculiar nature of the material – or rather, the spiritual – factors involved. Until I have managed to work out how Catholic beliefs are meant to work in terms of the religion as a whole, I feel I shall have to live with a measure of intellectual and spiritual discomfort.

I have decided to deal only with what I usually understand by 'Catholicism' – namely, the Roman Catholicism with which I have been familiar throughout my life: that is, the Western version of Catholic Christianity which is represented in the Roman tradition. I shall use the terms 'Catholicism', 'the Catholic tradition', 'Catholics' and 'the

Catholic faith', as it suits me, to refer specifically to that form of Christianity. Nothing provocative or condescending or exclusive is intended by this usage, adopted as it is simply out of my own convenience, as well as to ensure that I might know what I am talking about. Given my view of religion, as will appear, personal familiarity with a religion is of the first importance when there is a question of discovering what its beliefs are meant to mean, and how a religion may be supposed to work. I am aware that Catholic Christianity has come to be differently packaged in other particular Christian traditions; but with those I remain, despite considerable contact with some of them, still more or less unfamiliar. As an outsider I would not presume to offer an account of the way they claim to function as particular approaches to Christian 'salvation'. It just happens that they have not been such for me. It is obvious there is much overlap and a great deal in common among most, if not all, Christian traditions, despite the efforts of some Christians over the centuries to cut themselves off from their brethren. For the purposes of this book on Catholicism, I have chosen to think of the non-Roman traditions of Christianity as particular religions in their own right. It is for them to give their own account of themselves as ways or means of 'salvation'. However, what I want to say about Catholicism may still serve the better understanding of both them and perhaps even of other, non-Christian religions.

It is commonly claimed, often out of ignorance and laziness, that since there is only one God but many religions, all religions 'really' worship the same God; so that it matters little, if anything, which religion, if any, you belong to, since we are all going to finish up in the same place anyway. This strikes me as muddled nonsense which it is important to try to sort out. For one thing, I simply do not think it is sustainably true that the many religions all worship the same God. Scrutinize them closely and there emerge, I would say, as many Gods as there are religions. Nor does it help to say that the many religions are all 'really' worshipping the same one God in some way unconsciously and despite all their widely different approaches to religious worship and to life. Unconscious worship sounds to me like no worship at all. I think the nonsense is started by a shallow concentration on the systems which religions follow, by spotting what certainly look like similarities between them, and by then concluding that the religions in question must all amount to much the same thing. In this way the question of just what sort of 'thing' any particular religion is, is neatly avoided. But in any case, important as that question is, it is not so important as the question concerning the spiritual effects of a religion – just how does a religion work for the good – the personal and spiritual betterment – of its adherents? To answer this question is to get to the heart of a religion – to see through it as a religious system, and to discover its spirituality – what it has to offer human beings by way of 'salvation', by way of satisfying the native needs and aspirations of the human soul or spirit. At this deeper level religions differ immensely. Their systems may look relatively the same. As systems they may all centre on a God or gods. They may all be more or less organized and institutionalized. But how effective – and how beneficial – are their spiritual workings on humankind?

I would say, very roughly speaking, that there are at least two ways in which a religion may be viewed as working spiritually. In the first place, a religion works partly as a spiritual ideology, a body of visionary ideas, a theory, a more or less systematic basis for a certain distinctive way of viewing and thinking about the world and of living a certain kind of life in it. In the second place, a religion works partly by offering what is more properly called a spirituality, a means of fostering and regulating the growth of the interior life of the human spirit or soul or self, of spiritually enlightening the mind and motivating the will, of achieving an inner state of peace and 'salvation' and holiness. In fact these two views of religion usually interact with one another. Most often a religion remains an undifferentiated mix of both ideology and spirituality into which persons are born or converted, and

Prolegomena 9

with which, in a generally uncritical manner, they may or may not persevere throughout their lives. However, it is not difficult to understand how a religion might operate as no more than an ideology or simply to feed a personal and individual spirituality. We can all think of dangerous and fanatical instances of the former, and of perhaps impressive cases of the latter. It is the common mix of these seemingly uncongenial forms – an ideology and a source of personal spiritual life – which prompts the greater need for clarification. Institution and spirit seem doomed to exist in permanent tension. The question is: how are the two supposed to cohabit and cooperate?

We are familiar enough – perhaps too familiar – with the way religions work as ideologies. Here a religion imposes itself, controls lives, makes claims, touts for support, proselytizes, preaches its distinctive message, pursues its mission, makes promises (often of an unlikely kind), exercises its power and authority, demands conformity to its priorities and principles as well as more material contributions to its resources, regulates religious and moral and even secular behaviour, punishes transgression, expels dissidents, promotes and maintains its own self-interest over the good of its individual members – and so on. Its licence to act in these ways rests on its claim to be the authoritative possessor of a distinctive kind of truth, normally embodied in a more or less elaborate system of propositional beliefs which give expression to the distinctive world-view of the particular religion – the way it insists on getting people to see the world and the place humankind has in it, how the world as it sees it came to be, where the world is heading, what the world needs for its own eventual good, and where it is otherwise going to finish up. In fact, when it comes to the ways in which a religion works as an ideology, there may sometimes be no great difference between it and the more interfering or oppressive kind of secular state. This similarity may be deeply regrettable, but it has to be said that it is difficult to imagine how a religion could entirely lack an ideological component and still register its public presence and exercise its influence in history.

But it is also to a religion that many people still turn

when they are in search of personal spirituality – when they feel the need to foster or repair and renew that aspect of their lives which, however much it remains dependent on physical factors, they see as uniquely their own and 'internal' to themselves and distinct from material considerations and the intrusions of others – the interior life of the soul, the spiritual life. Here religion becomes a way for people to deepen their relationship with whatever God or gods they worship, in order to overcome their failings, to promote their personal godliness or holiness, to foster and increase their personal and moral integrity, to comfort themselves when struck with life's disasters, to learn to attend closely to life's more serious issues, to discipline the unruly motions of their minds and hearts and wills, their thoughts and desires and feelings, whether in order to bring them into some more devoted, more centred, more contemplatively attentive form of life, or to brace themselves for more effective activity in the direct alleviation of what they see as other people's needs. People look to a religion in this sense to supply them with spiritual power and energy, with models and motivation, with tested techniques of prayer and contemplation and self-discipline, with different modes and measures of commitment, with the opportunity of sharing their ideals and their efforts with others of a like mind, or of attaching themselves to a group or a community whose common purpose might further their own intentions. A religion provides a spiritual home and a support for those who take the life and 'salvation' of their souls seriously; and it leads and instructs and guides them towards the fulfilment of their spiritual goals. It comprises the community of those who find themselves called to the same form of 'salvation'; and in certain contexts a religion will gather itself together and form what might be called 'a church'.

Among the important questions raised by the co-existence or even 'symbiosis', of ideology and spirituality – or as I would prefer to say, of systematic religious *beliefs* and personal *faith* – in the followers of a religion such as Catholicism, there are at least two which seem to me to call for attention. First: is there any important connection between them which is perhaps essential to a religion and

Prolegomena 11

to the way it works? And second: if there is any real and functional connection between them, exactly what is it? Trying to answer these questions will involve asking others: just what does a religious ideology amount to anyway? What kind of meaning does it have? What might be its cognitional status? What kind of truth does it tell? How much does it serve to define human beings? These – and no doubt others – are the kind of questions I would like to address in what follows.

❧

But the form of such questions threatens to become stubbornly abstract, and I have in mind to write a personal essay which is meant to deal with the more practical problem of living with my Catholicism. Thus one of the important questions I need to face myself is whether I am looking for some final understanding of religious ideology or for a personal spirituality. Is a correct understanding of the *beliefs* of the Catholic system more important to me than my own Catholic *faith*? – or rather, since the two seem to be somehow inescapably entwined, of which of the two – understanding or faith – do I now, at this late point in my life, find myself more in need? This question I can answer without hesitation. I am more in need of faith – but it has to be a faith that I can also understand. My priority is to search for, and discover, a personal and spiritual understanding of my Catholic faith. I have lived a life as a Catholic which has never lacked for opportunity or effort to assimilate the religious ideology of Catholicism. In fact, some might well say that forty years in a religious order noted for a certain ideological firmness, and half those years spent teaching the disciplines of university theology, may well have produced the ideological overload which is precisely what is now aggravating my problem. As a Catholic I am prepared to accept that a personal spirituality is likely to come only with ideological strings attached; but – to change the metaphor – I feel sure that it is time the ideological tail stopped wagging the spiritual dog. To change the metaphor again: it will have to be a matter of correcting the balance between the two factors in favour of the spiritual, of asserting the importance of the spirit over that of the letter, of granting the spirit open access to the dry, scattered, doctrinal bones, letting the spirit flesh them out, clothe them with meaning and make them live: 'I will put my spirit within you, and you shall live, and I will place you on your own soil; then you shall know that I, the LORD, have spoken and will act, says the LORD' (Ezekiel 37:14). The time, I feel, has come for me to be placed on my 'own soil', to discover in myself, in such down-to-earth humanity as I share with others, those spiritual needs which my Catholicism is meant to fulfil.

I should try to explain why I need a corrective in favour of spirituality. The beliefs which constitute the Catholic ideology are theological in their expression. Whatever meaning they have they express in terms of God and his actions. Much of my problem I am inclined to put down to my once having been a jobbing theologian, and to the effects – they can be bad as well as good – which a career in theology can have on a person. After vigorously courting the Queen of the Sciences for more than quarter of a century, and with only occasional tiffs between us, I thought I had at last finished with her. I had developed critical views about her over the years we had been together; but by the end I had made a kind of peace with her, and I thought we had parted company courteously enough on the understanding that if she would leave me alone, I would leave her alone and get on with what I had come to consider better things. I did my best to fulfil my part of the bargain, but like a jilted and jealous partner, theology kept on nagging me for more of the attention I had once lavished on her. She is an exotic and difficult creature, given to portentous and prophetic utterance, subtly intuitive, wilfully imaginative, uncomfortable to live with, if only because the ultimate issues she raises are those which any serious person would not wish to ignore. But I would think it impossible to have a lengthy relationship with theology and not to have problems with her, with her tricky methods, her grand pretensions, and, most of all, her Sibylline gift for endlessly wrapping up truth in obscurity (*obscuris vera involvens*, Virgil, *Aeneid* 6.100). Perhaps it had been too early, and I had been too young, and she too old, when we first met: 'Theology after breakfast', says Wallace Stevens (*Les Plus Belles Pages*), 'sticks to the eye.' She may have infected me with religious cataract or spiritual myopia. But whatever my problem and her defects, Catholicism would be quite lost without her, as we shall see; there are still times when I feel privileged to have spent a good long time in her company.

But what I think is needed is a less abstract, spiritually more pragmatic approach to religions, and not least to Catholicism, in terms of how they are meant to *work* – that is, in terms of how they produce those effects in human lives which they claim are for their betterment. In making such an approach it is vital to recall that religion does not actually exist in general, and statements about it as a general phenomenon can be only abstract and are often speculative. Worse, such statements distract attention from the essential particularity of a religion, its specific spirit or genius, its characteristic notion of God – from most things, in other words, that it is important to appreciate about it. Doubtless broad statements about religion in general may be of some philosophical, psychological, sociological or even economic interest. They may help to indicate some aspect of religion's general connection with 'human nature' or with the human psyche or with human society or with the universal human prospect of death. But they really have little to contribute towards a practical understanding of how any particular religion actually constitutes a means or a method of 'salvation' and how it functions as such – how a particular religion is meant, in its own terms, to be effective in the improvement of the quality of human living. To be properly understood in this practical way each particular religion needs to be examined in terms of what it has to show for itself and what it has to say for itself – in terms, that is, of its inspiring and founding insight or vision, as well as of its own particular religious history and tradition.

Looked at from this more practical point of view, a religion can be described, still roughly speaking, to be a more or less organized approach to finding 'salvation' which has its origins in the spiritual insight or vision of some founder or reformer, has survived the obstacle course of history so far, and remains on authentic and public offer. Other descriptions will suit other interests and other opinions. William James famously took 'religion' to mean 'the feelings, acts, and experiences of individual men in their solitude, so far as they apprehend themselves to stand in relation to whatever they may consider the divine' (*The Varieties of Religious Experience*, lecture II). For the purposes of James' brilliant lectures (surely some of the best ever written) this served as a useful definition. But it has more to do with individual religious psychology than with what is commonly called a religion. It lacks the public and institutional dimensions that are called for in dealing with 'a religion' such as Catholicism; and it ignores the notion of 'salvation'. But I think my broad approach will suffice for my present purposes. Just what is meant by the central metaphor of 'salvation' can be left open for the moment, if only because different religions, Catholicism among them, are characterized by their own different views about what constitutes 'salvation' – and so, of course, by what they mean by 'God' – and about how that 'salvation' should be attained. On this showing, then, there will be as many particular religions as there are different approaches to 'salvation' on offer. Each of them needs understanding in its own particular terms – in terms of the 'salvation' it offers and of the way in which it goes about offering it.

The way in which a religion offers 'salvation' is tied to tradition – is 'traditional' in the strict sense that the offer is dependent on the extent to which the salvific insights of the original inspirer or founder have been effectively handed down over the years. In fact a religion and its tradition become practically interchangeable terms. There are as many particular religions as there are particular religious traditions. Without its own tradition, no particular religion would continue to exist. A historical tradition – the consistent effort at handing on the saving truth first realized by its inspirer, at effectively transmitting it and at ensuring its gradual 'inculturation', its appropriate development and elaboration, and its historical preservation and promotion – all this is what any particular religion essentially depends on. A tradition comes to embody all the ways in which a particular religion has come to understand and express itself and to further its salvific mission. These ways are often many and various, and their complex and interrelated development is historically traceable. Hence it is no surprise that a religion can normally point to a variety of schools of interpretation or movements within itself, to different spiritualities and different theological emphases, and to the developing histories of its moral teaching, of its liturgical and devotional practices, of its laws and organization, of its governance and its exercise of authority. As an approach to finding 'salvation', a religion is in fact a highly complex theological and cultural artefact.

Given such essential variety and complexity within the structures of any one particular tradition, it seems inevitable that a particular religion can become difficult to understand and interpret as a whole. Hence it is that the overall interpretation and understanding of it tends to fall conveniently into the hands of a favoured few, professional insiders, a clerical caste, who then become the main source for such understanding as they pass down to the rest of their less well informed co-religionists. This is one of the ways – there are others connected with worship and discipline – in which a particular religion can pass increasingly into the possession of the privileged sector of a 'church'. In such ways understanding a particular religion can rapidly become a matter of esoteric knowledge shared by few, and the possession of that knowledge can easily become a source of privilege and of power over the many, who naturally feel excluded from the higher reaches, and from the deeper spiritual meaning, of their religion. Hence it can also prove very difficult for ordinary insiders, let alone for outsiders, to understand how a particular religion is meant to work as a means of 'salvation'. The message from above will be: conform and trust the system. And increasingly a particular religion will be passed on as an institutionalized system, with an inevitable dilution or distortion of the spirit in which the religion was originally founded. Sorting out this ruinous state of affairs in order to get back to the original inspiration and the actual workings of a particular religion will become a Herculean task; and any serious attempt at understanding a particular religious tradition must therefore involve close knowledge and a lengthy and critically intelligent experience of it.

The historical, geographical and cultural spread of Catholicism over two millennia has ensured that it presents its offer of 'salvation' in elaborate and complicated ways. These comprise a rich and varied mix of traditional religious elements: different modes of divine worship, with the sacramental re-enactment of Christ's unique and exemplary self-sacrifice (the Eucharist or Mass) at their centre, a further six sacraments, different forms of personal and public prayer, a full range of liturgically structured services, a multitude of devotions directed to God, Christ, Mary and the saints, the reading, recitation or prayerful study of sacred texts, meditation, liturgical music, many styles of art and architecture, a wonderfully wide range of different forms of the committed or contemplative religious life, preaching, catechetical instruction, moral exhortation, codes of conduct, religious education, social teachings, an ingrained hierarchical structure and a clerical caste, authoritative leadership – to name only the most obvious traditional elements through which Catholicism has come to understand, maintain and express itself, and to practise what it preaches in its mission to offer its particular form of 'salvation' effectively to the world at large. It has built itself up into a complex system of traditional practices which are meant to enable it to exercise that mission. Many of these practices are not specific to Catholicism, but are to be found, often with altered emphasis, in other religions.

But I think it is both true and important to say that there is one element which, whilst it is by no means absent elsewhere, is often considered to characterize Catholicism to the extent that Catholicism is sometimes thought virtually synonymous with it. It is also an element which, unless it can be rightly understood, can dangerously distract from the spirituality of Catholicism. I refer to the way in which Catholicism's self-understanding has long been expressed and presented most formally in its doctrinal tradition – in its dogmas, as they are unflatteringly called, the traditional system of authoritative creeds and doctrines which Catholicism has developed over the centuries, not only by way of defining itself and its convictions and its mission more clearly, but also in order to quell controversy and dissent. They count as authentically valid expressions of how Catholicism understands itself as a particular approach to 'salvation'. I doubt whether anyone would deny that Catholicism has always presented itself as a 'dogmatic' religion; and many would base their objections to it on precisely this prominent characteristic. Others have found its dogmatic clarity the chief attraction in Catholicism, serving, as it may seem to do, as a rock of certainty in a tossing sea of religious doubt.

It appears to be the case that Catholicism has been passing through a phase, or a fashion, in which it has been trying not to emphasize its own dogmatic character to the same traditional extent, presumably in the hope of favouring other aspects of its salvific mission. Certainly the familiarity of Catholics, especially the young, with the doctrinal teachings of their religion has declined, it would seem, to a level not much above total ignorance. Popular books and sermons on doctrinal topics are rare. This decline in the attention paid to the Catholic doctrinal tradition may have to do, of course, with the contagious disparagement of teaching authority which is found in many walks of life; or, more particularly in Catholicism, it may have to do with a growing inability to appreciate the use and meaning of doctrine, or perhaps with the fashionable demand that more immediate and less structured forms of worship which lack doctrinal content should provide that intensification of the feelings that uncritically passes for 'religious experience'. But Catholicism, duly understood in the light of its own traditions, is a religion which offers a saving experience which, as I hope to show, not only fosters feeling and emotions, but also involves a disciplined and practical structuring of the imaginative intelligence and the restless heart – a fully human spirituality in the deepest sense. Catholicism is very much the product, after all, of some of the finest minds of late antiquity, the Middle Ages and the modern age. It bears their intellectual stamp, with its intelligently and imaginatively crafted framework of carefully articulated doctrines. It seems no exaggeration to claim that it is the doctrinal tradition that provides the backbone, so to speak, of Catholicism as a religion – maintaining its proper shape and its integrity, keeping its head and its heart in the right place and ensuring that its basic vision stays clear.

Whilst I think that fuller account of the doctrinal tradition of Catholicism needs to be taken in the understanding of Catholicism, I must also register three key and related reservations in its regard. Firstly, traditional doctrines must not be assumed to be purely ideological elements in Catholicism; secondly, they need to be seen as subserving the overall practical aims and purposes of Catholicism as a spiritual religion; and thirdly, the precise nature of their meaning and truth within the whole organic context of Catholicism needs to be properly understood. The restoration of the doctrinal tradition in line with these reservations is a tall order; but it seems right to try to understand Catholicism by concentrating attention on that traditional element which most characteristically and explicitly displays Catholicism's own understanding of itself – its credal and doctrinal tradition. I quite realize that, in assuming this stance, I must sound like a religious neo- or ultra-conservative bent on rallying the forces of reaction by banging the dogmatic drum. I can only promise, at this stage, that this is far from being the case. I have chosen to highlight the doctrinal tradition of Catholicism not only because it is an obviously salient and defining feature of traditional Catholicism which happens to have fallen into popular neglect, but also because it is only through knowing at least the more important elements in the doctrinal tradition, through understanding them sympathetically and coming to intelligent terms with them, that the way lies open for their radical interpretation and their practical reinstatement in Catholicism as a working salvation religion. I also choose to deal with traditional Catholic doctrines because I have no interest in expounding the meaning and the workings of Catholicism by trying to make it all up as I go along.

I do not think I should proceed beyond this point without issuing a stern Spiritual Health Warning. I do not intend to write a book for readers of a religiously nervous or squeamish disposition. I would strongly recommend that Catholics, or anyone else who finds the kind of questions I am likely to be raising about their beliefs unacceptably intrusive or biased or misleading or wrong-headed or upsetting or otherwise flawed, or who thinks my whole approach deplorable, should stop reading now. They should not outrun their own intellectual curiosity or undermine their personal certainties or disturb what precious peace of mind they think they have by trying to question their own (or anybody else's) Catholicism, as long as their own views happen to satisfy their religious needs. They might count themselves fortunate, and should persevere in their ways. But there will be others, Catholics and non-Catholics, who might feel ready to take a more adventurous look at Catholicism as a religious spirituality. Or there might be some who, for one reason or another, have already rejected Catholicism as meaningless and useless; and they might be prepared to revisit it, give it another chance, and take a closer look. I have really only one aim: to try to come to terms with my Catholicism in ways that may also make it more generally and more intelligently credible and spiritually effective.

It is helpful to note how there were times when St Paul felt he had to insist on a proper, fuller way of understanding the Christian message, and when he had to express his disappointment that his converts were, with damaging results, still managing to get it wrong. Paul had no time for such an immature response. 'Infant' in the New Testament is an interesting word. 'Infant' (*nêpios* in Greek, like its equivalent Latin *infans*, denotes an inability to speak or express oneself, a state of inarticulateness) comes over as a term of praise in the Gospels (Matthew 11:25; 21:1 cf. Psalm 8:1–2; Luke 10:21), where stress is laid on the need for a child-like reception of the Gospel revelation, as opposed to the hesitations of the adult sophisticate. But with Paul it is quite different: with Paul an 'infant' is someone who remains stuck at an undesirable stage of serious religious immaturity:

> What I am saying is this: the heir, as long as he is a *nêpios*, is no better than a slave, though he owns the whole property; but he remains under guardians and trustees until the date set by his father. It is the same with us: when we were *nêpioi* we were enslaved to the elemental spirits [or 'the rudiments' – or perhaps 'the scientific principles'] of the world.
> (Galatians 4:1–3, my translation)

Furthermore it was a stage of personal development which Paul himself had been glad to leave behind:

> When I was a *nêpios*, I used to talk like a *nêpios*, I used to think like a *nêpios*, I used to reason like a *nêpios*. Since I have become a grown man, I have shed what goes with being a *nêpios*. (1 Corinthians 13:11, my translation)

'Infancy' is a stage of religious development which other 'Pauline' writings also find an undesirable obstacle to the fuller understanding of essential religious teaching:

> About this [Jesus as high priest] we have much to say that is hard to explain, since you have become dull in understanding. For though by this time you ought to be teachers, you need someone to teach you again the basic elements of the oracles of God. You need milk, not solid food; for everyone who lives on milk, being still an infant [*nêpios*], is unskilled in the word of righteousness. But solid food is for the mature, for those whose faculties have been trained by practice to distinguish good from evil. (Hebrews 5:11–14)

What is more, religious infantilism indicates an instability which renders people vulnerable to deception – 'we must no longer be children [*nêpioi*], tossed to and fro and blown about by every wind of doctrine, by people's trickery, by their craftiness in deceitful scheming' (Ephesians 4:14).

Elsewhere Paul himself is at pains to explain more fully and clearly why infantile religious immaturity was dangerous and undesirable. A defective grasp of religious truth on the part of his immature converts rendered them susceptible to every kind of inappropriate interpretation. In a world where philosopher-preachers were many, as well as highly popular and influential, he directed: 'See to it that no one takes you captive through philosophy and empty deceit, according to human tradition, according to the elemental spirits [possibly 'the scientific principles'] of the universe, and not according to Christ' (Colossians 2:8). And he found it especially necessary to warn the Corinthian faithful against the worldly 'wisdom' which would serve to disempower the 'foolishness' and 'weakness' of God revealed in Christ crucified, who is 'the power of God and the wisdom of God' – 'so that your faith might rest not on human wisdom but on the power of God'. It was not in 'lofty words or wisdom' or 'with plausible words [or 'the persuasiveness'] of wisdom' that Paul preached the mystery and wisdom of his God, but solely in terms of 'Jesus Christ, and him crucified'. This amounted to 'a demonstration of the Spirit and of power, so that your faith might rest not on human wisdom but on the power of God'. So 'among the mature we do speak wisdom, though it is not a wisdom of this age', but 'God's wisdom, secret and hidden, which God decreed before the ages for our glory ... things God has revealed to us through the Spirit; for the Spirit', the very Spirit Paul has received from God, 'searches everything, even the depths of God ... so that we may understand the gifts bestowed on us by God' (see 1 Corinthians 1:17; 2:12 passim).

Only those who are themselves spiritually mature can receive these gifts of God's Spirit. Their reception requires a level of spiritual understanding which is plainly not to be found in everybody.

> Those who are unspiritual do not receive the gifts of God's Spirit, for they are foolishness to them, and they are unable to understand them because they are spiritually discerned. Those who are spiritual discern all things, and they are themselves subject to no one else's scrutiny. (1 Corinthians 2:14)

It is not for unspiritual 'infants' that Paul is writing when he writes in terms of the Spirit of God. He is not ladling out milk, but providing solid food for grown-up and spiritually adept Christians. He is thinking and writing on a higher level where the only way of understanding is spiritual, effected by God's own Spirit. In a tricky sentence he claims: '... we speak of these things in words not taught by human wisdom but taught by the Spirit, interpreting spiritual things to those who are spiritual' (1 Corinthians 2:13) – though this last phrase might mean 'interpreting spiritual things in spiritual language', or even 'comparing spiritual things with spiritual' (NRSV variants *ad loc.*).

Given the nature of what Paul understands by the divine Spirit, we can hardly expect to be able to define what he means by 'spiritual'; but whatever else he may mean, he must, it seems to me, mean at least 'non-literal'. Paul's concern was to establish that understanding his essential message required that his converts move into a new and higher mode of intelligent interpretation, away from an infantile literalism, and away from one which merely reflected the philosophical jargon of the day, towards one expressed in terms derived directly from 'Christ crucified, a stumbling-block to Jews and foolishness to Gentiles, but to those who are called, both Jews and Greeks, Christ the power of God and the wisdom of God' (1 Corinthians 1:23–24). It was the spiritual truth that this crucified and risen Christ stood for – the way he understood things, his whole mentality, his *nous* – that now alone mattered. For Paul it was quite enough to quote Isaiah (40:13), 'For who has known the mind [*nous*] of the Lord so as to instruct him?', and to flatly declare 'But we have the mind [*nous*] of Christ' (1 Corinthians 2:16). There can surely be no better model, no better method, to follow than Paul's for anyone intent on trying to clarify the understanding of the Catholicism to which he made such a foundational contribution. The proper understanding of Paul's message lies in the spiritual understanding of God and his ways that is native to the human mind of the crucified Christ.

My point in dwelling on the texts above has been simply to show that Paul held that it is vital in appreciating the meaning and truth of his new religion that it should be interpreted and understood, not only in a thoroughly adult and articulate manner, but also spiritually – in a way derived from, and consistent with, its spiritual content and purpose. Paul found that defective and immature understanding of a religion will seriously damage its saving truth. Now interpretation and understanding are intellectual procedures, and it seems that there is no substitute for them in any mature approach to a religion. We are supposed to think hard about our religion, to use our mental faculties of intellect and imagination to their fullest extent, in considering and expressing what it is meant to mean, how it delivers the kind of truth it has to tell, and how it works to bring about the salvation which it promises. But we are also to have minds and imaginations which can cope with the novelty of new approaches – which are not prepared to be confined to the habitual frame of mind we have been constructing since our spiritual childhood. We need to remain open to what might take us further and deeper – to be ready to think and imagine in ways which are consonant with, and controlled by, the particular spirit – or Spirit – of the religion in question. In the case of a religion like Catholicism which originates in the spiritual inspiration provided by Jesus, these ways will involve enquiring into what Paul calls 'the mind of Christ'. Such at any rate is roughly the route I hope to follow.

※

I can see that I cannot seek to discover the way Catholic beliefs are meant to be understood, and how they are to be connected with the salvific workings of Catholicism, without raising questions of a wider and deeper kind about Catholicism as a whole. For Catholics to say that there is a problem about the meaning of their religious beliefs usually serves as an indication that they are no longer willing or able to accept them without more ado on the say-so of their religious leaders, and want to give them up. I do not find that this is the case with me. As far as most of the faithful are concerned, their leaders have long taught them their beliefs at face value, taking little or no account of any further or deeper spiritual meaning and use that the beliefs might have; and most of the faithful have learnt to take it as a sure sign of unfaltering faith not to concern themselves with how the beliefs they are taught are meant to be understood. These simple positions are what I am no longer able to accept for myself. It is not that I find myself locked in disagreement with the Church authorities in matters of subtle interpretation. My problem is that the authorities seem so reluctant to interpret and understand Catholic beliefs spiritually at all. Perhaps somewhat perversely, it has been this failure that has firmly convinced me that there is much more to the religion and spirituality of Catholicism than the Church authorities commonly allow to meet the eye.

So gradually my view of Catholicism as a religious spirituality has begun to diverge from the Church's standard version of it. My problem with it is that, for one reason or another, the latter does not attempt to display the fuller and deeper picture presented by the traditional religious beliefs of Catholics – the full spiritual scope and depth to be found in them. Matthew's Gospel portrays Jesus as telling the uncomprehending crowds 'many things in parables' (13:3), and then explaining his meaning carefully to his disciples, before asking them: 'Have you understood all this?' (13:51). When they say they have done so, Jesus then draws the following conclusion: 'Therefore every scribe who has been trained for the kingdom of heaven is like the master of a household who brings out of his treasure what is new and what is old' (13:52). This evangelical model of teaching is not, I think, the one adopted by the Church authorities. That what is old in Catholicism should be taught is absolutely necessary, and, to my mind, is nowadays neglected; but it is also meant to be understood; and if the Church has fresh insights to impart, they should not remain locked away in some spiritual treasure-house in the Church's safekeeping.

But I realize that there is more at stake here than a simple distinction between two versions of Catholicism, the standard Church version and a version which I feel ought to be suggested, in which Catholic beliefs would be firmly taught, not just as a series of ideologically correct tenets, but as having a positive use and meaning as parts of a wider, more spiritual vision. The traditional system of beliefs is, as I have already noted, a highly public feature of Catholicism, and insiders are not slow to insist, and outsiders to remark, on the prominent part it plays in the life of Catholics. But the belief-system is, I am hoping to show, deeply and functionally embedded in the whole internal logic of Catholic spirituality, in the spiritual salvation which Catholicism claims to offer. Far from being a collection of museum curiosities which have accumulated in the cellars of Catholicism over the centuries, the traditional system of beliefs is, I am convinced, thoroughly and deeply organic to the spiritual workings of Catholicism. To isolate the system as a separate object of enquiry or investigation would falsify any hoped-for findings regarding Catholicism as a whole. It would lead to a failure to appreciate how other key features of Catholicism should be thought of – not least the nature of Catholic faith (which I shall treat as distinct from, but necessarily related to, the business of holding beliefs), as well as the function of the Church.

In all this I cannot disguise the fact that one thing I have been trying to do is to make a working distinction between Catholicism as a spiritual religion and the Church as its responsible operator or representative. The religion or spirituality of Catholicism is not to be simply identified with the way in which the institutional Church had chosen to package and purvey it. The institutional Church has its indefeasible part to play, certainly, in the true maintenance of 'what is old' and in the fresh presentation of it – in preserving and promoting the genuine article. It is what the Church exists to do. But there can still be so much to be discovered about how the beliefs which belong to Catholicism might be better understood. I think I can see how they might be capable of playing a key role in what could be reasonably expected of a religion – the spiritual truth which 'saves' humankind from itself.

The institutional Church, laden as it is with predominantly administrative and pastoral concerns, looks on the religion of Catholicism as a possession entrusted to it for conservation, a holy object, pearls, not to be given to dogs or thrown before swine (Matthew 7:6). It is a possession over which the Church has developed the authority to exercise powerful and efficient control. It can be offered to the faithful in simplified form for general consumption, a pre-fabricated, almost penny-in-the-slot system of salvation, delivered with carefully drafted instructions for its methodical use under proper supervision. But I began to see that for me Catholicism might be better treated more broadly as a humane spirituality than as a monopoly religious nostrum marketed by the Church. Of course, the Church would still have to be there in some form to serve and to service Catholicism, but some priority needs to be given to a more personal, more individual, more flexible, more imaginative and at the same time more practical understanding of Catholicism, in which a Catholic's religious beliefs would provide more direct access to Catholicism's characteristically spiritual appreciation or vision of the real human world. Catholicism might come to be seen as a general or common humane spirituality – a way of realizing humankind's immense potential for wisdom and goodness and holiness, of overcoming the selfishness and materialism, the resentment and the guilt, which so cripple all of us, of expanding hearts and minds and souls, of focusing people's attention on reality through faith, hope and love, and so leading them to the vision of their God.

᠅

The truth is I had begun to see rather more, and not less, religious and spiritual truth than generally meets the eye in the Catholic tradition of beliefs. I realized that, at some point, I would have to explore the tradition further and subject at least parts of it to more radical scrutiny. And I would have to do it on my own. This I was reluctant to do for several reasons. For one thing, I had many rather more entertaining things to do. Again, whatever I produced myself could hardly aspire, at least initially, to be much more than a piece of private interpretation. It could be no more, as I have said, than an essay in the strict sense – a personal, tentative shot at saying what I considered needed to be said. I was also aware that whatever I said was likely to be judged unacceptable and wrong by someone. So why bother with further exploration at all?

I put the whole business off for some years and got on happily with other interesting pursuits. But still some need to go through with my exploration of the Catholic tradition kept on imposing itself. Theology, that petulant Queen of the Sciences, would not leave me alone.

At some point a final settlement, a showdown, an *Auseinandersetzung*, had to take place between us. At the same time I was growing ever more convinced that there had to be much more to Catholicism as a religion than conformism with church requirements or confessing church creeds or the acceptance of church discipline. Not that I wanted to indulge in anti-church polemics or more futile calls for reform. I am by temperament what I would call a romantic conservative; and I am liberal, I hope, only in a generally humane sense – that is, when being liberal has little to do with politics or religion. What I favour is the imaginatively radical interpretation of traditional materials; and to be radical it is necessary to go back and grub about among their roots. Again, I began to feel that, although I no longer had any public responsibility as a teacher of theology, I still needed to come to terms myself with what I personally thought was the religious meaning of Catholicism. I still needed to make my own peace with what it was all supposed to mean to me. There was still that possibility of achieving something like 'final belief'. So in time I reluctantly set other matters aside and proceeded with as much honesty and clarity as I could bring to the task as I saw it. If others were going to think my findings 'wrong', then so be it. I knew well that my search was likely to take me into realms where words would have to work, so to speak, under extreme conditions – where their usual literal writ no longer ran, and where they would have to be consistently exchanged into the foreign currency of metaphor, or be put to constructing stories and fables or narrating myths; where reason would remain essential, but would soon reach the end of its sense-bound tether; and where the creative imagination would be the only faculty that could hope to penetrate, however obliquely, the spiritual mystery that I felt sure lay at the heart of Catholicism. To be over-concerned about 'right' and 'wrong' would be to show a lack of courage, and to misconstrue the personal, not to say the wholly tentative, nature of what I wanted to do. I was somewhat heartened by a remark attributed to A. J. Ayer: 'Why should you mind being wrong, if someone can show you that you are?'

I felt reasonably confident about my technical qualifications for the job I had in mind. But I need to be frank from the start of this book about my personal stance. I follow St Paul in thinking that no properly spiritual understanding of Christian truth will be dependent on a particular school of philosophy; not because I have a low opinion of philosophy – in fact, far from it – but because understanding Catholicism does not seem to me the sort of thing which can be promoted by the adoption of any particular secular school of thought, although some eclectic acquaintance with philosophical schools and their methods may help. But no religion is to be understood in philosophical terms – any more than it could possibly be understood in scientific terms. Understanding Catholicism will depend on viewing Catholicism in its own right and its own light as the kind of spiritual religion it happens to be. All the same, understanding can hardly start from cold. Some stance, some position has to be taken if there is to be any kind of intelligent engagement with the matter in hand. This is true even when the stance or position is a negative one: that is, one consisting in a refusal to share certain familiar or accepted philosophical platforms.

So among the many other defects which will be noticed in this book, the way in which I distance myself from certain philosophically based positions will be obvious. I propose being, in variously qualified senses, agnostic, atheistic and positivistic. To write a book on Catholicism that sets out both to emphasize the strict limitations – indeed the positively 'unknowing' character – of our knowledge of the divine, and also to deny that theism is the philosophical system which provides anything like an appropriate understanding of Catholicism, will be considered by some to be a surefire way of shooting myself in both feet. But I also further insist on appearing to shoot myself in the head as well by ruling out the literal meaning of those theological expressions of Catholic belief which might be thought metaphysical. This positivistic stance is intended to leave me with a Catholicism which will look more like a humanistic spirituality than a conventional religion – a way towards the practical spiritual knowledge of the truly human mystery which enlightens and governs ordinary human lives, and which I shall continue to call God. If readers find this just too much to stomach, then I could have no objection if they laid – or threw – this book aside now. But I recall how the wise and saintly Eric Mascall, quoting Etienne Gilson, once described the ideal theologian as combining 'a perfect intellectual modesty with an almost reckless intellectual audacity'. I would like to think I was at least trying, in my small way, to aim at this ideal – though I am far from suggesting that the Dr Mascall I fondly recall would have agreed with my approach. But I must explain myself in more detail.

What I call the agnosticism of this book is necessary because in my view the salvation which is offered by Catholicism is not to be achieved through esoteric intellectual enlightenment or through the liberating acquisition of the certain knowledge (or *gnôsis*) of some transcendent Beyond where Catholics may hope to find, after shedding the sad encumbrances of the material existence they have to endure in this life, an everlasting and spiritual home after death. Such a view of salvation (which is perhaps not at all uncommon) is strictly 'gnostic'; and along with a studied contempt for the physical or bodily aspect of humanity, the way of achieving it is known as 'gnosticism'. Catholicism, interestingly, had to confront the temptation to become gnostic from the very start of its long history, and its earliest theologians vigorously condemned gnosticism as a completely false and most dangerous heresy. My kind of 'a-gnosticism', therefore, is called for, because I suspect that many Catholics (and non-Catholics) are tempted to think that in order to be saved Catholics must hold on, with literal certainty, to a body of esoteric beliefs (a 'creed' or a series of dogmas) which theologians, early and late, have concocted, and which the Church authorities impose on them. In other words, that ideological correctness, or what is thought to be 'orthodoxy', has salvific power in itself, and perseverance in maintaining it with certainty, along with the routine overcoming of sin and trying to be good, guarantees salvation in some Beyond.

This attitude, I think, is markedly gnostic (with more

than a touch of Roman Stoicism); and I wish to counter it by being agnostic – by reminding myself that what I can actually know, in any direct or strict sense of the word 'know', about anything outside the confines of our world is – nothing; that Catholic beliefs do not express factual knowledge, although orthodox beliefs still remain crucial to properly Catholic faith; and that all religious language needs to be taken reverently with a large pinch of critical salt – not because it is meaningless or non-truth-bearing, but because it must be accompanied with a consistently critical appreciation of what it can possibly mean, and of how it means it, if it is to produce its properly valid religious and spiritual effect.

As for my 'a-theism', this is, of course, no rejection of the ultimate mystery which we are, in our limited state, constrained to call God. Rather, it is an attempt to bring God back into the Catholic picture. My atheism is a denial that the philosophical system of theism is best or uniquely suited to express the mind and heart of the Catholic religion. On the contrary, it seems to me that for seriously thoughtful people theism throws up just those obstacles which serve to block a broader and more spiritual understanding and appreciation of Catholicism. I am not saying that philosophical theism does not have its uses. When Catholicism first appeared, in a world where polytheism was common, a strict monotheism was called for; and it was contemporary theism, with its one, absolute God who is infinite in all perfections, and who obliterates the need, and indeed the possibility, of any other god, which lent its support to the Catholic position. But its powerful and elegant development in medieval Catholic thought canonized what was still at root a pagan theism, and gave it a permanently central controlling role in Catholic theology. As a purely philosophical 'grammar' of the abstract idea of a unique God – absolute, omnipotent, omniscient, omnipresent – theism can hardly be bettered. If one happens to be determined to think of God as an infinite entity or object, theism lays down the rules that have to be kept in doing so, and describes the essentially divine qualities required. It tells us, rightly, what existence – if such a God were ever to exist – would entail for such a God. But the abstract idea, let alone the existence, of an absolute personal entity of this kind cannot be said to suit Catholicism, whose God, after all, is believed to be truly represented by the ineffable mystery of the divine Trinity 'personally' involved in the creation and salvation of the human world – and what is more, intimately and personally related with all humankind, a God whose perfect and final revelation was an individual human being, Jesus of Nazareth. Much of my engagement with Catholic theology seems to have amounted to little more than a pointless struggle to force the saving mystery which is the God of Catholicism into the Procrustean bed of theism – an attempt to square theological circles or solve factitious conundrums. My adoption of a-theism is a rejection of the misleading philosophy of a God who cannot be the God of Catholicism, even if he were actually to exist. If Catholicism is ever to be better understood as a spiritual religion, the God of theism has got to go, and a radically re-imagined God has to be sought for in the only place where that God is believed to have fully revealed himself.

I am also opposed to any literal interpretation of metaphysics. I must confess that, whilst I can fully appreciate metaphysics as an imaginative attempt to come to terms with how actual things exist by attributing various abstract principles or categories of 'being' to them, I cannot accept the existence of metaphysical entities – those principles or categories of 'being', in other words, considered as actual existing things themselves, as 'reified'. To choose an example at random: 'matter' and 'form', like 'substance' and 'accident', belong to a brilliantly imaginative way of analysing the process whereby things can be thought to change and yet somehow remain themselves. We try to account for the fact that actual things can change and still be the same things by choosing to think – imaginatively, metaphysically – of their forms or their accidents changing, while their matter or substances remain the same. (The all-too-famous Catholic doctrine of 'transubstantiation' deftly employs this philosophical analysis in reverse by asserting that, while the accidents of the Eucharistic elements remain the same, their substance changes.) But matter and form, substance and accident, are not *things* which exist as such or as real entities in themselves. They must not be 'reified' into material objects. They are abstract metaphysical categories of 'being' which have been invented (originally by Aristotle) to help us out in the imaginative, necessarily pictorial, understanding of things and the changes which things undergo. 'Metaphysical' does not mean that they actually exist somewhere beyond or behind or even somehow within the physically real world, or that they form some subtle or immaterial part of the physical constitution of real things. It means that they have no actual physical existence at all, but simply provide us with an intelligent way of understanding physical reality that happens to suit the limitations of our minds and appeals to our imaginations.

This refusal to accept the existence of metaphysical entities on my part extends also to the God proposed by philosophical theism. Hence my atheism, mentioned above. I do not believe that the God of Catholicism is best identified with a metaphysical principle or entity, and I would deny the existence of such a God, not only because I do not hold that metaphysical principles or entities exist, but also because I do not think that Catholicism, as a religion, 'works' or makes sense, as I have said, in terms of such a God. The God of the Catholic religion must be a spiritual, not just a philosophical, God. A theistic God, the supreme metaphysical fiction, seems to me precisely what the God of Catholicism cannot possibly be, for all the efforts of theologians to make the theistic idea of God fit into the religious and salvific role played by what Catholics are meant to mean by God. Think of the endlessly sterile theological debates about the 'incarnation' of a theistically conceived God (let alone of one 'person' from a theistically conceived Trinity), about the 'problem' of evil when a theistic God is supposed to be absolutely omnipotent, or about the inevitable tussle between divine grace and human freewill – not to mention the even more important matter of the distress that the idea of an essentially immutable and inexorable theistic God can cause to suffering human minds and hearts.

Nor is it acceptable to say, as is often said or assumed:

'But such difficulties simply point to the fact that God is mysterious'. The mystery of what we mean by God cannot be made dependent on our own intellectual incapacity to solve problems we have ourselves invented. There is all the difference in the world between a mystery and a problem: the former is infinitely and permanently beyond us, the latter evades solution, often because we have expressed the problem in wrong or misleading terms, or because we happen to have insufficient evidence to solve it. But none of this means, of course, that I am denying the intense reality of that mystery which, as I shall claim, envelops and defines the experience we have of our own personal human existences, and which we are constrained by our own limitations to continue to call 'God'. 'God', I would say, is the name which Catholicism forces us to give the intense reality of our own personal human mystery, once we have been led to pay serious attention to it. In fact, the mystery we call God turns out to be the most real thing about us.

It is my rejection of gnosticism, of theism, and of the cruder forms of metaphysics that will clear the ground for re-imagining God: for imaginatively understanding God anew as the name for the reality of the mystery of our own humanity. I want to restore that mystery to the role I believe it has as the leading idea of Catholicism, and this means first moving those problem-causing positions firmly aside. I have given this book the title 'On Re-imagining God', because I consider this is exactly what needs to be done before the spiritual riches to be found in Catholicism can be brought to light and appreciated. I have long thought that the most important and revealing question to pose, especially to oneself and perhaps to other people who will not be upset by it, is: 'So what kind of God do you actually believe in then?' The reason for its importance is, not that any of us is in any position to define what God is like, but because the kind of God we choose to believe in (or not) is what most clearly defines us as the kind of human persons we are. Answering the question calls for the intelligent use of the creative imagination; and what I have been trying to make clear is that certain habitual or conventional ways of imagining God do not, in my view, work for Catholicism. The spiritual mystery of the Catholic God needs to be radically re-imagined in line with Catholic tradition; and this means going back to its inspired roots in Jesus of Nazareth and reviewing what the central Catholic doctrinal tradition both says and means.

There are advantages in expressly reverting to the intelligent use of the religious imagination rather than continuing to hide behind some philosophic mind and its reach-me-down, second-hand system. For one thing, the chances of simply setting up some alternative cast-iron orthodoxy are diminished. Imagination is individual and free, and therefore already focused on a spiritual and personal interpretation of Catholicism. For another, it leaves the field open for anyone else who wishes to try their hand at re-imagining Catholicism, its God and its salvation, in some better way. The kind of mystery I imagine the Catholic God to be is that mystery which doggedly accompanies the attentive contemplation of my ordinary human experience of actually existing as a human person, a mystery which is unmistakeably real, infinitely impenetrable, endlessly inviting and all-encompassing – the permanently obscure but lucidly clear revelation of all that we cannot grasp fully about ourselves. I have much more to suggest about this mystery later, and I shall contend that we encounter it best when the humanity which we have in common with Christ becomes more like his in the course of the death-bound lives we live among our fellow-humans. It is in this way that we are to find what Catholicism calls God, and thereby be granted our salvation. In other words, my view of Catholicism and the salvation it offers is that it works after the manner of a humane mysticism which centres on the spiritual core of the very same humanity which it pleased God to make his own.

༺༻

It may be reassuring for those who are disturbed by the re-imagining of the mystery of God in terms which differ radically from the concepts of classical theism and which draw on the existential experience of our own humanity to point to what I believe is a familiar and traditional example of re-imagining God's mystery for the purpose of expressing precisely the intense kind of intimacy between God and man which Catholicism posits, and which plays an important part in the expression of what Catholicism understands by salvation – a way which in fact was used in the Old Testament before it took on the extended meanings called for by the New. Bear in mind that, in this field, we have to work more with the constructs of the imagination than with definitions worked out by the mind on principles derived from elsewhere. Reliance on the latter would preclude the very sense of mystery which it is so necessary to evoke in any account of what is worth calling God. Nonetheless I sympathize with the desire for as much imaginative clarity as is possible in the circumstances. It is only reasonable that people should look for some really useful and meaningful metaphor for the kind of re-imagined God I am proposing. It seems to me that there has long been such a metaphor in use, not far to seek and from a source which should occasion no surprise. I refer to the biblical metaphor of glory.

Glory (*kabôd*), the biblical lexicons say, generally means weight, heaviness, importance, success, worth. In God's case it comes to mean the reality of his mysterious presence or his appearance (hence the rather flat Greek translation of it as *doxa*), visibly manifested in cloud or fire or in some other way, as being too bright for man to see directly – God's evident but mysteriously obscure reality. But God's glorious reality is impenetrable, not through any inherent obscurity, but through an excess of luminosity, brilliance, light. To 'give glory to God' is to confess and express the sheer reality of the divine, to acknowledge God's mystery. But it is when the established metaphor of divine glory strikes the imaginations of the theologians of the New Testament that we find it put to new and telling use. For Paul, looking back at his past, the old metaphor of glory has now taken on a completely new life:

> Now if the ministry of death, chiselled in letters on stone tablets, came in glory so that the people of Israel could not gaze at Moses' face because of the glory of his face, a glory now set aside, how much more will the ministry of the Spirit come in glory? For if there was glory in the ministry of condemnation, much more does the ministry of justification

abound in glory! Indeed, what once had glory has lost its glory because of the greater glory; for if what was set aside came through glory, how much more has the permanent come in glory. (2 Corinthians 3:7–11)

The glory which once served to express the mystery of God has now been eclipsed by the greater glory which expresses the new revelation of God's mystery which was inaugurated in Jesus. God's mystery has to be re-imagined in terms of the glory of this man who is now the prime and unique glorifier of God in the new dispensation: '... so that God may be glorified in all things through Jesus Christ' (1 Peter 4:11). It is in him, his humanity, and in what he went through, that the true glory of God's mystery is now to be discerned – in Jesus 'who for a little while was made lower than the angels, now crowned with glory and honour because of the suffering of death ...' This crowning glory was not to be confined to himself alone, but was granted 'so that by the grace of God he might taste death for everyone' – everyone, that is, who shares his way of being human and his attitude to human life and death, and thereby stands to share in the perfection of his glory, since 'it was fitting that God ... in bringing many children to glory, should make the pioneer of their salvation perfect through sufferings' (Hebrews 2:9–10). Glory now becomes a metaphor for the contact-point, the interface, through which humanity comes to know and share in the mystery of God. For this spiritual encounter to be possible, not only does God need to be re-imagined, but so does our humanity as well. The re-imagined God graces humankind with his glory, and then the glory of being human becomes a participation in God's glory, and thereby of God's mystery. Glory becomes a vividly operative metaphor for the new relationship between God and humankind inaugurated in Jesus.

For this truth to come to fuller expression, we have to draw on the metaphorical and mystical dimensions of the baptism which first unites us with Christ. Hence Paul declares:

> Therefore we have been buried with him by baptism in death, so that, just as Christ was raised from the dead by the glory of

the Father, so we too might walk in newness of life. For if we have been united with him in a death like his, we will certainly be united with him in a resurrection like his ... if we have died with Christ, we believe that we will also live with him ... So you also must consider yourselves dead to sin and alive to God in Christ Jesus. (Romans 6:4–5, 8, 11)

Divine glory, then, – here 'the glory of the Father' – is used as a metaphor to express how the mysterious reality of God impacts on us in the new dispensation. Divine glory expresses the reality of God's mystery which we can now come to share, if we confront and undergo this precarious, death-bound life of ours with the faith of Jesus: 'since we are justified by faith, we have peace with God through our Lord Jesus Christ ... and we boast in our hope of sharing the glory of God' (Romans 5:1–2) – 'if, in fact, we suffer with him so that we may also be glorified with him. I consider that the sufferings of this present time are not worth comparing with the glory about to be revealed to us' (Romans 8:17–18), when 'the creation itself will be set free from its bondage to decay and will obtain the freedom of the glory of the children of God' (Romans 8:21). This comes about when Christ 'will transform the body of our humiliation [or 'our humble body'] so that it may be conformed to the body of his glory [or 'his glorious body'], by the power that also enables him to make all things subject to himself' (Philippians 3:21) – a process of spiritual transformation which takes place as 'all of us ... seeing the glory of the Lord as though reflected in a mirror, are being transformed into the same image from one degree of glory to another; for this comes from the Lord, the Spirit' (2 Corinthians 3:18). But spiritually transformative as it may be, the process of our achieving our share in Christ's glory, far from taking us out of our physical humanity, is imagined as taking place at a thoroughly human and 'bodily' (or physical) level – though as far as the dead are concerned, we have to leave it to God to provide a suitable body where this transformation into glory can take place: 'there are both heavenly bodies and earthly bodies, but the glory of the heavenly is one thing, and that of the earthly is another' (1 Corinthians 15:40, and see 35–49).

To claim that the use of the metaphor of glory enabled a New Testament theologian like Paul to offer some account of the new approach to a re-imagined God inaugurated by Jesus seems right; but some have thought that it was that other notable theologian, the author of the Fourth Gospel, who first attempted to do so on a more comprehensive scale. His Jesus actually represents the glory, the mysterious veiled reality, of God's own cognate Word or self-expression, living and dying as a human being among us, offering 'signs' of his inward glory to those with faith to read them. The whole Gospel draws on and develops the belief that 'the Word became flesh and lived among us, and we have seen his glory, the glory as of a father's only son, full of grace and truth' (John 1:14). Indeed it may be possible to suggest an understanding of this endlessly intriguing Gospel in terms of the Father's Spirit at work in bringing the human glory of Jesus his Son to its fullness and perfection in the paradoxical emptiness of his death on the Cross, the supreme point where his glorification is finished, and the point from which his glory becomes transmissible through the same Spirit to those who follow him in faith. Hence Jesus' cryptic dying words on the Cross, 'It is finished' – it has been completed, perfected – at which point 'he bowed his head and gave up his Spirit' (John 19:30).

Prior to Jesus' own utter glorification on the Cross, for all Jesus' passionate desire to give the Spirit to his followers, his sharing with them of the divine Spirit which glorifies humanity, was not possible:

> Jesus ... cried out, 'Let anyone who is thirsty come to me, and let the one who believes in me drink. As the scripture has said, "Out of the believer's heart shall flow rivers of living water."' Now he said this about the Spirit, which believers in him were to receive, for as yet there was no Spirit, because Jesus was not yet glorified. (John 7:37–39)

Hence Jesus is drawn eagerly towards 'the hour' of his glorification, declaring on his final entry into Jerusalem, 'The hour has come for the Son of Man to be glorified' (John 12:23) in his death, an event which will at last enable his followers to be taught and reminded of everything by 'the Advocate, the Holy Spirit, whom the Father will send in my name' (John 14:26), to get the point of what Jesus stood for; because 'his disciples did not understand these things at first; but when Jesus was glorified, then they remembered ... ' (John 12:16). It is this eagerness of Jesus that is embodied in his great prayer to the Father for his disciples before going out to Gethsemane: 'Father, the hour has come; glorify your Son so that the Son may glorify you ... I glorified you on earth ... So now, Father, glorify me in your own presence with the glory I had in your presence before the world existed ... All mine are yours, and yours are mine, and I have been glorified in them ... The glory that you have given me I have given them ... I desire that those also, whom you have given me, may be with me where I am, to see my glory, which you have given me ...' (John 17:1, 4–5, 10, 22, 24).

Both Paul and John use the metaphor of the glory of God to express the reality of God mysteriously revealed, no longer in cloud or fire, but in the suffering and dying and risen humanity of Jesus, which is ours as well as his; and at the same time as the reality of God spiritually communicable to us, if we approach human living in the Spirit of Jesus the Son. Paul says that now Christ has been 'raised from the dead by the glory of the Father ... the life he lives, he lives to God ... so you also must consider yourselves dead to sin and alive to God in Christ Jesus' (Romans 6:4, 10–11). Or as John's Jesus puts it more bluntly: 'The glory that you have given me I have given them' (John 17:22). The glory of God now stands, not for some awesome communication from God, but for mysterious but communicable divinity itself – a re-imagined Godhead. In Jesus' case, through his life, suffering, death and resurrection, his humanity inherits – comes into possession of, becomes charged with – the glory that is proper to the Father's Son and also eternally his by divine right. It is this same glory that, in our case, is given and shared with us by divine grace and favour – and in both cases spiritually, through the working of the Spirit. Hence we are enabled, to the extent that we reflect the human glory in which the Father raised and glorified Jesus, to be spiritually, mystically, progressively transformed into his likeness 'from one degree of glory to another; for this comes from the Lord, the Spirit' (2 Corinthians 3:18). The humanity we have in common with him stands to be transformed, through the Spirit of Jesus, into a vehicle, a transmitter, of the glory of God. We worship and glorify the Father through the glory which is the gift of his Spirit to the humanity we share with his Son. It is through this human glory of ours that we stand to increase God's glory through the way we live and die (*ad majorem Dei gloriam*).

I think it can be seen even from this brief and very rough excursus on the biblical metaphor of glory that there might be developed a comprehensive and deeply trinitarian theological picture of the new reality in which the followers of Jesus are meant to exist. But more of this later. All I am trying to suggest at this point is that in the biblical use of glory we have a powerful and traditional metaphor which has served to express the re-imagining of God and our union with God – and that therefore we have no reason to shrink from a similar re-imagining of God if it is found that a spiritual understanding of Catholicism may be helped by it. I would maintain that there is a serious need for Catholicism to re-imagine God if it is to be true to itself as a spiritual religion. It is not possible to express the intense intimacy, the sheer closeness, between humanity and God which a duly understood Catholicism entails by conventional recourse to the metaphysical abstractions of classical theism. Indeed the God of theism may be fairly said to be the result of imagining God as the conceptual antithesis of humanity. This consideration alone should rule it out as a way of coming to terms with the God of Catholicism. It needs to be remembered that if the basic Catholic doctrine of the Incarnation is to be in any way meaningful, it must be at least congenial for the God of Catholicism to be as human as we are. Catholicism needs a God with whom human beings are enabled to engage in a mutual interchange of glory.

☙

I have by now revealed that the kind of spiritual understanding of Catholicism which will alone do justice to it as a religion requires a move into the field of mysticism and the mystical. I have made this move, distancing myself from the gnosticism, theism and literally understood metaphysics which commonly bedevil accounts of Catholicism, because I am convinced that Karl Rahner's remark that the Christian of the future would either be a mystic or nothing is profoundly true. Mystery, mysticism and mystics have, sometimes deservedly, got themselves and religion in general a bad name, indicating the deliberate pursuit of obscurity, esotericism, secrecy, mystification. But the words are properly used of a direct or immediate communion or contact with what a religion refers to as its God, a communion which is incommunicable in literal terms. It cannot be directly described or accounted for in words. Humanly contrived methods and systems may play their part in our making progress towards achieving such communion, but they do not in the end constitute it. Communion between mystics and their God is intimate and personal, cutting out 'the middle man' from the communion experienced. Hence the Catholic Church has not looked on mysticism with much general favour – and with some reason. Self-proclaimed mystics need watching. They can become a law unto themselves. They are likely not to conform to average Catholic behaviour; and for their communion with God they do not count themselves dependent solely on what the Church authorities provide by way of worship, teaching, sacraments, rules and discipline. Because mysticism emphasizes individual and essentially incommunicable experience, mystics are not easily controlled within the body of Catholic believers. Hence the Church has either dealt rigorously with mystics who have emerged from her ranks, and, where they have proved genuinely irrepressible, ensured that they have been officially adopted and carefully domesticated. The mystical factor in Catholicism has been consistently played down; and mystics have generally had to prove themselves through their outstanding holiness of life, for which, after their deaths, the Church has not been slow to claim the credit. In other words, Catholicism has often been prepared, though reluctantly, to license mysticism in special cases, but it does not tend to see itself as a mystical religion. It does not see itself as what might be better called a popular mysticism or spirituality.

It may be the case that Catholicism, too bent on presenting itself as intellectually respectable or simply as the popular choice, has been too slow to acknowledge its own inherent mysticism or spirituality, and has thereby, at least in Western culture, eventually begun to lose its essential appeal as a religion. It is, after all, safer and easier to opt for emphasizing the institutional system at the expense of the spirit, the method at the expense of the inspired intuition, the literal, material understanding at the expense of the spiritual and metaphorical. Such an emphasis, if carried too far, can reduce a religion to a mindless compliance, and even to a form of institutionalized superstition. So in this attempt at a spiritual understanding of Catholicism I shall be trying to correct that emphasis by stressing what I believe to be the spiritual or mystical quality of Catholicism as a religion.

But I need to say more about what I understand by mystery and the mystical, and about their role in understanding Catholicism. That a religion should be grounded in the mystical should really come as no surprise; and it seems to me high time that these generally abused and debased words – mysticism, mystery, mystical – were boldly restored to their proper usage in the understanding of religion. They are commonly used, of course, where there is an inability or a refusal to provide a rational account or justification of knowledge – where there are pretensions to mystification, to mystifying others, to privileged knowledge of the intriguingly obscure and baffling, of the enigmatic, of the insoluble and inexplicable, of the secret and esoteric and arcane, and even of the sinister. They have thus become words which naturally rouse a strong, and often justified, suspicion of dubious nonsense, to do with anything from popular horoscopes and unsolved murders to 'the mystery of the universe'. Now, as I have already said, a mystery is far from being just a particularly tricky kind of problem. Problems differ from mysteries in that they can be solved, at least in principle; whereas mysteries surpass any possible explanation or understanding. The native usage of mysticism, mystery and mystical is, however, religious; and in the field of religion, these are words that are meant to deal, reasonably and wisely, with the evident limitations of our thoughts and words when we encounter what we experience as real but which remains inexpressible. Far from indicating a regrettable drift away from the factual, the words are meant to cope with what is all too factual to the religious mind and imagination – too factual to be caught in our ordinary concepts and expressed in our ordinary words.

Ludwig Wittgenstein famously ended his *Tractatus Logico-Philosophicus* (1922) with the words: 'What we cannot speak about we must pass over in silence' (7) – acknowledging that not everything we actually experience or feel as real can be adequately caught in the net of a system of thought and a language which is suited to dealing with the world of what we commonly acknowledge to be ordinary facts and states of affairs. Just before this he had made other lucidly cryptic statements regarding our experiences:

> It is not *how* things are in the world that is mystical, but *that* it exists (6.44).
>
> To view the world *sub specie aeterni* is to view it as a whole – a limited whole.
>
> Feeling the world as a limited whole – it is this that is mystical (6.45).

As he saw it, there comes a point 'when the answer cannot be put into words', and so 'neither can the question be put into words ..., [since] if a question can be framed at all, it is also *possible* to answer it' (6.5).

The solution does not lie with adopting a sceptical stance:

> Scepticism is not irrefutable, but obviously nonsensical, when it tries to raise doubts where no questions can be asked.
> For doubt can exist only where a question exists, a question only where an answer exists, and an answer only where something *can be said* (6.51).

> We feel that even when *all possible* scientific questions have been answered, the problems of life remain completely untouched. Of course there are then no questions left, and this itself is the answer (6.52).
>
> The solution of the problem of life is seen in the vanishing of the problem. (Is not this the reason why those who have found after a long period of doubt that the sense of life became clear to them have then been unable to say what constituted that sense?) (6.521).
>
> There are, indeed, things that cannot be put into words. They *make themselves manifest*. They are what is mystical (6.522).

A *catena of* statements such as this needs no commentary here: what it needs is long and meditative attention. Wittgenstein is not, of course, dealing with religion, but with inexpressible matters which, though they could not be accommodated in his earlier philosophy, still impose themselves on our experience, and may not be dismissed out of hand. They simply *'make themselves manifest'* – show or reveal themselves. Sceptical doubt is ruled out as a response, because it presupposes that there could be an expressible answer which, in the case of the mystical, there cannot be, since we do not even know what question it is right to ask.

For me, this approach is called for by the obviously limited nature of our powers of understanding and expression. Wittgenstein is scrupulously leaving room for the occurrence of mystery and the mystical in experience. The proper response to it – though he shows no interest in the religious application of his views – comes down to what I can only call a kind of faith: that is, to a mystical attitude of acceptance towards the inexpressible truth of what reveals itself to be the case. It is this link between a kind of faith and the kind of secular mysticism about which Wittgenstein is speaking that encourages me to think that religious faith as such has also to do with the mystical; and that the mystical would be the right point from which to begin to try to explain Catholic faith. That the mystical might provide the right starting point from which to consider any religion can, in any case, hardly be surprising.

I have introduced Wittgenstein simply to show how mystery and mysticism can be intelligently handled by a philosopher who was devoutly positivistic at the time – though his later works are surprisingly rich in insights which illuminate many key aspects of religion, and not least of Catholicism. But it still has to be said that few Catholics would expect an account of their religion to begin with talk about mystical experience. Talk of mysticism, mystery, the mystical would strike them as altogether too outlandish, too impossibly far-fetched, to be worth considering. In standard Catholic teaching mystical experience is gratuitously vouchsafed by God only to spiritual adepts of long standing, and then only to a minority of those. To make mystical experience the common starting-point as belonging to the very essence of Catholic faith is to turn the tradition of Catholic spirituality upside down. This tradition insists that the pious soul must ascend slowly and painfully through various levels of purification and enlightenment on its path towards an encounter with its God, who might eventually deign to bless it, in rare cases, with a mystical experience of his Godhead. On this difficult journey, there is to be no bypassing the sacramental and disciplinary life of the Church.

But – and this is of key importance in my intended approach to Catholicism – I am not speaking about the mystical experience of God *as an object*. I have already confessed that I do not accept the theistic notion of God as a metaphysical entity; so for me mystical experience cannot involve experience of such a being, but rather of that re-imagined mystery which surrounds our humanity and which we are – for want of a better name – constrained to call God. Now as far as I can see, this mystery imposes itself on us to the extent that we decide to take our experience of existing in the world as human beings seriously. I am talking about the absolute mystery, the mystical, as experienced in the sheer fact of our actual existence as human beings, and as revealing its obscure presence in that existential fact. It is important to reject the way in which our minds have been falsely conditioned to think of the mystery and the mystical, simply because they are (so to speak) by definition beyond or outside us, as somehow distant from us, and therefore difficult to contact. Much intellectual and spiritual damage, I would say, has been wrought by the wrong use of the word 'transcendent' with its overtones of 'a Beyond'. This is damage that is not easily repaired by then having to talk about what is 'immanent'. There is no need to posit any literal beyond or outside or inside in order to make sense of our ordinary world – that limited whole which is open to the scrutiny of the human arts and sciences. What I am saying is that the mystery, the mystical, is best considered as a given and defining quality of the actual existence of our ordinary world, an existential quality which reveals itself when that world is rightly and attentively approached as the limited whole in which we actually exist. In individual terms, it is in and through our common ordinariness, properly felt and appreciated, that there is revealed the absolute mystery which inescapably belongs to each one of us, the mystical which surrounds and defines our experience of our human existence. Mystery, the mystical, mark the limits, define the boundaries, of the sort of beings we happen to be. We belong to true humankind as individual persons to the extent that we see ourselves enveloped and defined by the mystery, the mystical, which in religion is called God.

We need to dissociate ourselves thoroughly from the notion that mysticism is a highfalutin matter. It is, on the contrary, a fundamental aspect of being human. It can be operative in the most ordinary and common of experiences, where it serves to make those experiences real. At the most available level, mystery is what we can each encounter in our existential experience of our own personal humanity. Entailed in this experience there is an encounter with an irreducibly real, concretely factual, absolutely impenetrable mystery – to which a religion such as Catholicism gives the name God. The mystery consists in the sheer fact *that* – nothing to do with how or why! – we each exist as the human beings we experience ourselves to be – the sheer experienced fact of our individual personal human identity. This can only properly strike us as totally mysterious. The reason why it does not generally do so is that we simply do not give the mystery involved in experiencing our own existent, concrete humanity the attention it demands and deserves. Indeed we make sure we distract ourselves from it for much of the time. Hence the religion and spirituality of Catholicism, which arose, in my view, when a unique and exemplary human being succeeded in passing on to his followers the urgency of giving all their attention to the mystery which lay at the heart, not only of his own inspired experience of his own personal humanity, but also, if they but followed him, at the heart of their experience of the humanity they held in common with him. It is also my conviction that, because of its basis in the radical humanity of its original inspirer, no religion is better able than Catholicism, duly understood, to bring people to recognize that it is the demanding mystery of their own humanity that defines and explains them – to recognize, in short, that the Kingdom (or Sovereignty) of God is 'in fact ... within you' (Luke 17:21).

Catholicism seems to me to make spiritual sense only along the lines of the radically human approach I intend to take. Ultimately this approach is not so much my choice as that of Catholicism's inspirer, at the heart of whose mission to 'enlighten the whole of humankind [*panta anthrôpon*]' (John 1:9, my translation) lay a profoundly realistic knowledge of humanity, 'because he knew all of them, and ... he had no need for anyone to inform him about humankind [*peri tou anthrôpou*], since he himself knew what was in humankind [*en tôi anthrôpôi*]' (John 2:24–5, my translation). It is the mystery of our common humanity that was uniquely embodied and revealed in Jesus of Nazareth, and which has lain ever since at the heart, and confronted the mind, of the religion he inspired. It is, as I shall hope to explain, his profoundly human faith in the mystery of his own humanity – along with the hope and the love associated with that faith – which remains the uniquely normative and salvific human response to the mystery; and it is that remarkable human artefact, the belief-system of Catholicism, which is meant to give such faith, hope and love a proper imaginative and visionary background, and a setting, a limited whole, within which they can effectively operate. I would suppose that if it is our own humanity which is the ground and source of the mystery which surrounds and defines us, the place where our God dwells among us, then to approach Catholicism from some divine point of view would be tantamount to a retreat into obscurantism – to try explaining the obscure by the yet more obscure (*obscurum per obscurius*). So my approach, which tries to expound what I understand by Catholicism and how I think it is meant to work, will be from this radically human point of view; and I shall begin with faith as the proper human response to the mystery of our humanity.

☙

I make much of certain distinctions as I proceed, and it is on the validity of these that the usefulness of what I have to say will greatly depend. I have, for instance, already distinguished between the institutional Church as Catholics know it and the Catholic religion which is meant to embody their inherited spirituality. As a religion, Catholicism is spiritual – its work and its priorities have to do with the healing and growth of the human spirit through bringing it into communion with its own inherent mystery which it calls God. The Church, in the man-made form in which we know it, exists to preserve and promote the work of Catholicism – to make the spirituality of Catholicism credible and effective. Catholicism and the Church seem to be simply distinct kinds of things. But it is equally obvious that they belong together. They are plainly not meant to be wholly independent of one another. Without the creative and supportive efforts of the Church, the spiritual religion of Catholicism would not have survived in intelligible and effective form over the centuries. But a Church uninspired by the religious and spiritual purposes of Catholicism might as well be dead. They are, but in different measure ('asymmetrically'), interdependent. The earth-bound institution depends entirely on the spiritual, whereas the spiritual remains a wind which 'blows where it chooses, and you hear the sound of it, but you do not know where it comes from or where it goes' (John 3:8).

This initial distinction leads on to others, some of which are more basic than others, but all of which involve maintaining a clear difference between what must be ascribed to the sphere of the spiritual and what must be considered as belonging to the human efforts to come to some intelligible terms with it. To my mind this initial distinction licenses and validates a further radical distinction between analogously interdependent factors which I have used in what follows – the distinction between faith and beliefs. Faith is, obviously, an attitude of the spirit, whereas beliefs are man-made statements which believers are meant to confess in support of their faith. The implications of this distinction determine my whole interpretation of Catholicism, and I shall take care to explain myself in due course. At this stage I simply want to lay a few more of my cards on the table, or put down a few markers.

Whilst I have no time for the literal interpretation of metaphysical concepts and statements, I need them as imaginatively metaphorical ways of coming to understand the world – as interpretative constructs, stories, myths which enable us to know, to the extent that we can know, the mysterious reality which confronts and defines us. Insofar as Catholic beliefs seem to refer to a metaphysical world beyond or outside the physical world in which we have to live and die, I consider that they call for radical reinterpretation as religious metaphors and myths which structure and support the religious vision of reality to which our faith is our personal commitment. There has been much talk about 'demythologizing' Catholicism and religions in general. Let me say that I am strongly in favour of vigorously 'remythologizing' them, since I see no other way of understanding what they say and how they work.

There is also, perhaps, need for a word on my preferred approach to theology through its language. Not that such an approach reduces theology to a game with words, as some always like to think. Nor, of course, does it amount to denying that there is any such thing as a recognizable reality out there. All I am doing is simply making the commonsense distinction between the real and the ways in which we have to cope with it, not least when it is too real to be adequately understood in the language we have available. I have no argument with what we ordinarily mean by reality or the world, if only because there is nothing I can do about it. It exists, it is fortunately becoming increasingly transparent to properly scientific enquiry, it continues to create philosophical and scientific problems; but most importantly for me, the fact *that reality, and our individual human reality, is there at all* is what presents the abiding mystery which remains at the heart of Catholicism.

Catholicism contrives to impart its truth in various ways – worship, the liturgy, its reading of the Scriptures, preaching, and so on – but not least in the official, doctrinal language it has learned to use in the furtherance of its traditional self-understanding and saving mission. It uses words which are functional – they are used with a specific purpose, and it is from out of that purpose that their actual meaning can be read and their truth discerned. So to embark on an attempt to interpret and understand Catholicism without a closely critical awareness of the words and language it uses would be, to my mind, a serious miscalculation. Words and language are what indicate how Catholicism hopes to get people to try to cope with the mystery of their own reality. They do not substitute for reality: they interpret reality by way of offering the best kind of access Catholicism can offer to the saving truth about the mystery of ourselves – the mystery we all have to live with. But words like 'God', and about 'God', pose special difficulties, and it is necessary to address them.

Catholicism is strictly monotheistic, and has long represented its God, as I have already said, in the inappropriate form of the God of philosophical theism – a unique, absolute, transcendent divine entity who is both personal and infinite in all his powers, attributes and qualities. This essentially pagan kind of God does not square with the God of mystery involved in the Catholic view of salvation, as we shall see. But the theistic notion of God has some uses, not least in its assertion of what we refer to as God's transcendence and infinity. These imposing words, which always need to be used with great caution, are no more than the best we can do to give some inadequate expression to the essential mystery of whatever might be worth calling God; and they do it in the only way open to them – by their inherent denial of limitations. After all, transcendence, theologically speaking, means no more than being in no way confined or reducible to the limitations of our world; and infinity means being completely incommensurate with those limitations. Neither word has anything positive to say about the mystery we call God. Both words do no more than remind us that we can never hope to get our minds round that mystery. They are our way of putting down markers which are meant to preserve the mystery which confronts us. Paradoxically, it is in their way of saying what God cannot possibly be that they take us as far towards the mystery of God as human thought can go. The mystery of God remains intact, wholly beyond us. With God we are not only up against the limits of the ways in which we can think: we are also (and it amounts to much the same thing) up against the limits of the range of such words as we can meaningfully and positively use. We look out (so to speak) from our limitations as if towards a realm of strictly or literally unknowable reality where our minds do not reach and the writ of our language simply does not run. In other words we are confronted with what is properly and strictly called 'mystery'. With a highly verbal religion like Catholicism, whose doctrinal tradition has been so linguistically sophisticated and expressive, it is all too easy to forget this.

So does it make sense to speak of 'God' at all? (The inverted commas simply signal that we have a permanent language problem.) Two remarks are called for: first, it would be impossible to try to give any account of Catholicism as a particular religion – as offering an approach to 'salvation' – without reference to 'God', since for Catholicism 'salvation' has its source in 'God'; and in fact its basic understanding of 'salvation' is in terms of sharing the mysterious life of 'God'. Second, there is no reason why it should not make reasonable sense to speak of a God who transcends all finite reality, *provided we remain fully aware of just what we are getting ourselves involved in, and of what we are trying to do; and provided we also remain consistent in the way we consciously think and speak of 'God' as meaning the mystery which encompasses and defines our humanity.* This proviso, it seems to me, is crucial to the whole enterprise of understanding Catholicism and how it works as an offer of 'salvation'. We must consistently respect the limits, the finite scope, of the language we have to use to say what we mean. As far as the meaning of 'God' is concerned, words can take us only so far – only as far as an infinite and transcendent mystery can permit them to go – and after that, whilst we have no alternative but to go on using them, we have to realize that the words are out of their depth, and that we are using them by deliberately stretching, extending, adapting their meaning beyond their ordinary and literal usage. To fail to see, or to try to ignore, this problem which confronts our thoughts and words when we are dealing with the mystery we have to call 'God', is to make room for two errors which are fatal to a spiritual religion: first, the terminal error of technical idolatry – the literal reduction of the infinite mystery called God to the limited confines of our own thought and speech; and second, the all-too-common error of vulgar superstition.

We are all accustomed to use the word 'God' as a noun which either names or refers to some objective and infinite entity. But 'God' is neither an object in our literal sense of the word – otherwise God would just another part of our world of objects – nor the name of such an object, nor just another entity among the entities which are commensurate with our natural way of knowing. If God were just another object or entity, he – though of course gender simply does not come into it – would be measurable on the same finite scale as the rest of our finite objective world, and so could not be infinite. If he were not infinite, he could not be what we are trying to mean by 'God'. This does not at all mean that the mystery we have to call 'God' is not real, or that it does not – to make more unavoidable use of language which strictly speaking only befits objects – 'exist'. It simply means that the reality we use the noun 'God' to stand for is infinitely beyond the scale of objective reality we can perceive and understand, and even beyond what we literally understand by 'existing'. It means that our saying the word 'God' indicates, to the best of our limited ability, our awareness of the presence of an infinite, transcendent mystery – a mystery we must learn to maintain and respect in all that we think and say that has to do with 'God'. We have to learn to drop the sort of literalism that tries to invade mystery and simply generates problems. We have to learn not to take literally what we can only, at best, be trying our best to imagine – or re-imagine. In doing that, far from making God less real, we would be indicating to ourselves that the mystery which is God is more real than we can ever hope to come to terms with.

For instance, a common error is to imagine 'infinite' as meaning 'big', or even 'very, very big'. But of course it means nothing of that sort – at least in theology, although science may not aspire to the same rigorous standards of language usage. 'Infinite' has nothing whatever to do with size at all, which is only one of our measurable categories. Being infinite is a negative: it means not being subject in any way to any of the finite categories we habitually use to understand the things of our world. When we use 'big' in relation to what is infinite, we are not really thinking – we are letting our feelings take over and run out of critical control. 'Infinite' points to mystery, and the best we can do with such a mystery, in order to make it possible to think and speak about it, is to call it 'God' – and to remain consistently aware that nothing we can say about that mystery can be taken literally. Of course, if 'God' is believed to have revealed something of his own mystery – a belief which is clearly central to Catholicism – then our stance will be altered; but even then we have to remain aware that when we speak of 'God' we are still dealing with an infinite mystery, and still in given human terms whose literal range still remains firmly finite. At any rate, I feel I have insisted sufficiently for the moment on this crucial point to permit me to drop the irritating inverted commas which I have been applying to the word 'God' (and to 'salvation', as a divine initiative), although they will, of course, have to be strictly retained in the mind.

It will be necessary to maintain this cautious and consistent mental reserve in the use of religious language primarily because it is demanded by the transcendence and infinity of God; but also, in the present context, because of the origin and nature of the many theological statements which have made Catholicism such a markedly verbal and articulate religion. It has expressed and defended itself freely from the start in theological terms – in terms, that is, of God and of his sovereign intentions, his creative actions, his inspired words, his salvific intervention in human history through his Word, his ongoing offer of universal salvation and his eventual judgement of humanity. The theological language of the Catholic doctrinal tradition is thoroughly – and, of course, necessarily – anthropomorphic. Catholicism has sought to impose its own characteristic shape on the infinite mystery it has to call its God in order to be able to speak meaningfully about its God at all. There is nothing questionable about this inevitable procedure; but it puts the Catholic believer and interpreter under the obligation of never forgetting that in speaking meaningfully about the God of Catholicism they cannot be speaking literally. They are speaking theo-logically about an infinite mystery – in other words, in terms of a *theos* or God, and thereby doing the best they can with words which meaningfully prompt their minds and imaginations, whilst at the same time admitting that their words fall infinitely short of the mystery they are trying to express. There is no avoiding this infinite shortfall. It has to be lived with and worked through. Theologians constantly need to tell themselves to Watch Your Language, to Mind the Gap. The best that theologians can hope to do is to avoid misleading others by remaining aware of the inherent limitations of their craft; and in particular by avoiding the creation of those bogus problems, puzzles and conundrums that have so long bedevilled their efforts when they have supposed that they can endow the language of their theological craft with literal meaning.

This warning having been firmly delivered, a more positive, less forbidding view of the doctrinal and theological language which Catholicism uses to express itself and its mission as a religion of salvation might be framed by saying the language of Catholicism can be properly understood only in its own right: that is, in terms of the way it is actually used in the Catholic tradition itself – in terms of the way the language is meant to function in the overall logic of the Catholic system. It is a fundamental mistake to suppose that however familiar and common the use of a certain word may be in different areas of human discourse – for example, the word 'creation' as used by theologians, by artists and by scientists – it has a single common meaning, although its various uses obviously display some family resemblance. Human beings are capable of putting the same word to different uses, and of meaning quite different things thereby. Some would say that human beings are in fact precisely characterized by their ability to be creative with words and their meanings in this way. Doctrinal and theological language is strictly technical language, and it needs to be consistently understood in terms of the creative doctrinal and theological tradition to which it belongs. To assimilate the strictly technical meaning of its words to that of the same words in other language fields is a misleading abuse. But that Catholic theological language is an 'in-house' product belonging to the Catholic doctrinal tradition need not thereby render it any more hermetic or esoteric or private or misleading or untruthful than any other systematically developed technical language: for example, the language of chemistry or botany. Difficulties associated with doctrinal and theological language are bound to arise when it is understood as having a meaning which is independent of the creative intellectual and imaginative theological system in which it has been traditionally used.

Of course, in all this we still need to recall that if theological language were to pretend to literal or descriptive meaning, it would falsify itself, since such meaning must fall infinitely short of the transcendent mystery of God and his actions which it is being technically employed to express. To remain useful or meaningful, no theological language may be deemed exempt from this systematic inadequacy. It is deeply regrettable that taking religious language literally or descriptively (at 'face value') has come to be called 'fundamentalism' – a form of religion which generally has nothing more fundamental about it than an entirely superficial and self-deluding way of understanding religious (and especially scriptural) texts. This refusal to think serves only to get religions of all kinds a deservedly bad name. But worse than that: failure to appreciate the non-literal and non-descriptive nature of theological language is no venial mistake. It amounts, as I have already said, to the ultimate religious error, or 'sin', of idolatry, and it usually generates all manner of superstitions.

Given, then, that the doctrinal and theological language of Catholicism cannot possibly bear a literal interpretation, the only kind of meaning it can have must be, to speak very broadly, metaphorical. There are other descriptions of this kind of oblique, or 'slant', way of meaning. It might be classed as the mythopoeic, involved in creating myths or stories which contain the truth to be imparted; or as symbolic, that is, as using words as conventional signs to express itself; or as analogous, that is, we understand something we do not know directly by comparing it with something we do know directly. Catholic theologians have long had recourse to complex forms of analogy – to analogy of attribution, intrinsic or extrinsic, and to analogy of proportionality, for instance. My problem with them is that where they might be helpful, inherent in the act of comparison, it seems to me, lies a standing invitation for what might be called a 'creeping literalism' to infiltrate theological language. And certainly few Catholic theologians, having agreed that the language they use is analogical, have been prepared to stick to the rules which accompany that fact. The temptation to suggest that they have somehow acquired clear and direct knowledge of God is too strong. So it seems to me that 'metaphorical', broadly understood, both covers and explains what is happening when we use words to express, as best we can, the human mystery round which the religion of Catholicism has formed.

The metaphorization of ordinary language, its transference and adaptation to novel theological usage to enable Catholicism to express itself must be traced to the creative work of the human religious imagination. Human understanding, of course, comes in many different shapes and sizes, and one of the chief reasons for this appears to be the fact that humankind possesses a wide and highly personal range of types of imagination. The role of imagination in knowing and understanding, or – to put it another way – the cognitive function of the imagination, seems to me to have been seriously neglected by philosophers, no doubt intent on establishing as high a degree of impersonal or pseudo-scientific objectivity as they can for their theories. Hence factors considered as subjective and variable as the imagination are excluded from their interest. But the stubborn fact seems to be that it is individual human imagination that largely determines how things are known and understood in the first place. Faced with what may seem to be the same problem or object, one man's rigorous understanding of it may be judged a self-deluding fantasy by another. Failure to give the imagination a constitutive role in human knowing and understanding needs to be reversed. It cannot be that the human imagination is a neutral faculty which simply serves to provide materials for the higher intellectual activities of what we call the human mind; that the dictum *'nil in intellectu nisi quod prius in sensu'* – all the contents of the mind have first to come through the senses – is mechanistically true. The very way in which the senses and the imagination are brought to bear on the materials in the first place will dictate what use, what meaning, they may have for the mind to work on. It is for this reason that I have given such a leading role to the imagination in the understanding of Catholicism. But then I have to expect that other people, differently endowed, will understand Catholicism differently. They will think my approach – as I have confessed – to be romanticist rather than classicist. But to my mind (and imagination), there is no understanding Catholicism (or perhaps any religion) without assigning to the imagination a constitutive role in the formation of its teachings.

What this amounts to in practice is this – it enables me to say that although much Catholic doctrinal and theological language appears to consist of technical expressions (for example, incarnation, grace, predestination), this in no way alters the radically human status of those expressions, or reduces the imaginative inventiveness of their metaphorical adaptation to their novel usage and meaning in Catholic theology. We have been conditioned to suppose that theology has its source in some form of privileged access to the divine – it is sometimes even called 'divinity' – but this is to obscure the fact that it is a human craft, perhaps not altogether unlike art or music criticism, which seeks to express creatively those supra-linguistic matters that lie beyond the normal reach of the words we habitually use. Under proper critical control, the craft of theology can be developed by study and practice. Its metaphorical and imaginatively inventive quality in no way implies, of course, that theological language is therefore vacuous in content and in meaning. On the contrary, it is precisely that quality, critically maintained, which ensures that the Catholic tradition remains aware of the infinite mystery of what it means by God, and works under the influence of that mystery. Faced with the essential mystery of all that concerns God, the Catholic tradition must acknowledge both the complete inadequacy of attaching any literal or descriptive meaning to its doctrinal and theological language, and at the same time recognize the complete necessity of using such language as the only language humanly available to it. In a word, the discovery of the meaning of Catholicism, of its traditional doctrinal and theological self-expression, will depend on the consistent exercise of the theological craft of interpretation.

But given that Catholic doctrine and theology are the creative product of imaginative interpretation, what, precisely, are they an interpretation *of* ? On what are the imaginative skills of the theologians being exercised? Not, evidently, on some head-on, objective knowledge of the mystery which we call God. This mystery, as we have said, lies beyond the grasp of the human mind, and can only be approached obliquely, slantwise, indirectly, by the metaphorizing skills of the imagination. But what is there for the imagination to work at – to make the object of its metaphors, to come to cognitive grips with? The only answer I can offer to such questions is to say that what I think the Catholic theological imagination works at is the interpretation and expression of the experience we have of our own mystery-bound humanity as viewed in the light of the humanity of Jesus. Thus viewed, our humanity permits us to discern that our humanity possesses an inherent need for a 'salvation' which is not to be found simply in itself. Thus viewed, being human is seen, not as a matter of being a closed and self-sufficient system, but, mysteriously, as open and engaged in the constant search for amendment, improvement and fulfilment, an endless response to the call of its own mystery, which it is constrained to call God. And it is in the light of this demanding mystery that Catholic theologians elaborate a metaphorical picture – better, a vision – of reality which seeks to give colourful and meaningful expression to reality in terms of God and his actions. In other words, what Catholicism exists to develop and promote is a particular and distinctive religious vision of humanity and humanity's world.

Not, of course, that Catholicism and its theologians came somehow to invent the vision in the first place, as we shall see. The vision it exists to develop and promote claims to have its unique and ultimate basis and sole criterion in Jesus of Nazareth's own experience of being human – in his personally paradigmatic experience of the mystery involved in human life and death, an experience which Catholicism calls on all humankind to share. Jesus' personal experience of being human in the world prompted him both to complement and correct the religious vision he had inherited in his native Judaism, and to begin to elaborate a new vision which would be distinctively his own. What Jesus did was to re-imagine God, and it is his re-imagining that we have to seek to appropriate. His newly re-imagined vision involved the faith, hope and love which were evoked in him through the way he personally confronted and plumbed the mystery of his own humanity, the mystery on which he felt existentially so dependent that he characteristically addressed his mystery as 'Father'; the new vision came to expression through the creative use of his inspired interpretative powers and his deeply human imagination. For all this there seems to me to be abundant evidence in the New Testament. In other words, the Catholic doctrinal tradition and the dramatic vision of being human in the world which it pictures should be seen as representing a centuries-long attempt to be true to its sole foundation in the faith and the theological imagination of Jesus. But more of this later.

※

The real question I am posing remains one that few ever seem to ask themselves: namely, 'how is my religion (in my case, Catholicism) actually meant to work anyway?' The question is likely to sound too threatening or too irreverent or too flippant or too smartly critical or simply too inappropriate to many of those people already committed to the comforting certitudes which they derive from an unquestioning adherence to their particular religion. But it strikes me as a serious question, and I cannot see why it should not be seriously posed. That is, given that what characterizes a religion is some kind of offer or promise of 'salvation', just how is a particular religion meant to make that offer or promise good? I mean this how-question to be taken in a strictly pragmatic sense – as if I were asking an engineer how a steam engine works, or a magician how he does this or that trick. I would expect the engineer to provide a clear and convincing explanation; and as for the magician, I know that for all his legerdemain and cunning equipment, his smoke and mirrors, there is always a practical explanation, often distressingly simple, without which his trick would not work and he would be a useless magician. Of course, I realize that a religion is neither engineering nor magic; and with a serious phenomenon that belongs to the realm of the human spirit, a realm of spiritual insight and vision and 'spiritual exercises', such a practical how-question may seem at first oddly out of place. Yet if there is to be any hope of giving the claims of a religion to offer 'salvation' some credibility, surely it must be fair to ask the practical question of how exactly we suppose it does it. In posing this question I intend only to try to make the religion of my choice – Catholicism – more credible than it currently is.

Prolegomena

It is not as though most religions themselves, or at any rate their theologians, have been slow to suggest explanations of how the 'salvation' they offer may be thought to come about. But their suggestions must strike most uncommitted people as far-fetched. To take a fairly average account of how most Christian religions are thought to work: its saving efficacy is commonly thought to involve and depend on a sequence of metaphysical actions and events – in other words, on actions and events strictly independent of our natural world (hence technically called 'supernatural'), but still somehow effective within it – in which a God of infinitely remote qualities first creates the world and mankind to people it. But mankind, from the start, consistently fails to come up to divine expectations; so God, infinitely merciful and loving for all his infinite remoteness, sends his divine Son into our physical world for a time so that he might offer himself as a sacrifice to God on behalf of all mankind, a divine and therefore universal and infinitely efficacious act which makes up for all the deficiencies mankind cannot itself overcome, and in this way God saves them – or at least saves those who somehow accept the divinely self-sacrificial Son as their Saviour. This is no more than a very crude account of how a religion like Christianity is commonly thought to work as an offer of 'salvation'. But this kind of explanation of how Christianity works as a 'salvation' religion is really no more than a theological construct which presents a colourfully dramatic portrayal of 'salvation' in religiously mythical terms acted out on a metaphysical stage. A being from the divine sphere briefly dips his toe into our sinful physical world, nobly pays for it with his life, dramatically rises from the dead and returns to the divine sphere, and thereby – somehow – earns 'salvation' for all who are prepared to acknowledge what he has apparently done for them. But the really puzzling aspect of all this is that our 'salvation' has strangely little to do with us. It involves our sinful humanity only vicariously and passively, since our 'salvation' is predominantly a matter of negotiation or transaction between divine 'persons' in the metaphysical sphere, even though one of them spent his brief human life in our sublunary world. The practical achievement of our 'salvation' is dramatically located elsewhere in the Beyond.

But what is more important to note is that such an account offers no practical explanation of the actual working of our 'salvation'. It does not explain what is thought to be happening to us here and now as we are supposedly becoming saved. It adds no real meaning to our world, and brings no added value to it. What such an account offers is a vividly imaginative drama of 'salvation' set on a metaphysical stage in theological dress. But far from condemning or even criticizing it on those grounds, I shall go on to maintain that a theological account has its essential, but different and non-explanatory, part to play in the preservation and promotion of the Christian message of 'salvation'. But crucial as it is to the preaching of Catholicism, I have two major problems with it. First, as I have said, it does not amount to the kind of explanation an enquiring mind might justifiably seek. Surely there is something more to be said about the way 'salvation' is actually meant to work on the ground, so to speak – at the individual, personal and spiritual level. Second, and especially nowadays, such an account is certain to be dismissed as without value by those who see metaphysical (and therefore also theological) language as being nothing more than nonsense. What I shall try to explain is that theological language can not only make sound metaphorical or mythical sense, but that it is also precisely in that way that it is crucial to the spiritual vision which the faith of Catholicism proposes and which plays a practical and organic working role in the way the 'salvation' offered by Catholicism becomes effective. I think this is the kind of understanding that serious believers in Catholicism deserve and should be helped to seek. It is an understanding which will give a proper status and function to the system of theological beliefs which is so central to Catholicism.

Chapter 2
Faith

Whoever wrote the elegant New Testament document entitled 'To Hebrews', with its strictly alternate passages of theology and exhortation – and for whatever reason – clearly had an intense interest in a basic religious experience called faith, and in attracting certain followers of the Jewish religion towards sharing it. This interest peaks in the eleventh chapter, which begins with what amounts to a description of the experience of faith which sounds almost Aristotelian in its brevity. A recent translation reads:

> Now faith is the assurance of things hoped for, the conviction of things not seen. Indeed, by faith [*or* by this] our ancestors received approval. By faith we understand that the worlds were prepared by the word of God, so that what is seen was made from things that are not visible [*or* was not made out of visible things]. (Hebrews 11:1–3, variants)

The translation is accurate enough; and it carefully retains the opacities in the Greek. I offer the following translation, which I think is more transparent and more reader-friendly, though I would still count it as accurate:

> Faith is what gives our hopes their reality – it supplies an argument for things we cannot see. It was for having this [faith] that older generations received approval. It is faith that makes us realize that the way worlds ['the aeons'] are constructed depends on God's decree, with the result that what we can see is not simply made up of what appears to be the case.

Obviously I have relaxed the terseness of the passage. I have paraphrased a little, and then only to bring out what the passage seems to mean. I have not, I think, taken any undue liberties with the Greek.

What I find most striking here is the way in which the experience of traditional faith is said to create what it then takes to be real. The faith-experience is creative, positively constructive. One might say that without this faith-experience there is no future and nothing really worth seeing; our worlds remain in disarray, and all there is to see are mere appearances, impressions. In our experience of faith our hopes take on substance, we can see beyond appearances, and worlds assume a divinely decreed structure and shape. Faith plays an active and imaginative, not to say creative and constructive, role in the way people who have faith are led to see and understand the reality of their world. It would hardly be an exaggeration to say that this religious faith, which inspired generations of Jews, is, in its way, wilfully counter-intuitive; but it would be more aptly described as *visionary*. It aims at providing the background support that is needed by our hopes for the future, affording sight of the invisible, and seeing reality, not as it simply appears to be, but in the light of the difference God makes to it, and of the construction God is thought to put on it. But there is another quality that also belongs to this kind of faith – it is, strictly speaking, *mystical*. It purports to offer a form of direct, unmediated contact with what inexpressibly escapes the ordinary catchment of our unaided mind and senses – with what belongs to the realm of God. In other words, this faith is a spiritual response to religious mystery.

As I have said, there will be those who suppose that in introducing the visionary, the mystical and religious mystery into an account of faith, I am, from the very start, opting for an irrational approach to the Catholicism which I want to explain – that I have, all too literally, taken leave of my senses. I would agree that in a way this is precisely the case. In fact, I am making this early move in order to establish my view on the only grounds on which, as I think, a convincing account of Catholicism and its workings can be based. Fundamental to Catholicism is the kind

Faith

of faith-experience sketched in the Hebrews passage because, as I hope to show, Catholicism is the religion of the human spirit. It is a spiritual religion which works spiritually. It is not the materialistic salvation system to which some, promoters and enemies alike, have sought to reduce it. It seeks to address the innate shortcomings, the worst sufferings, and the highest aspirations of humankind by offering support which enhances and boosts the spirit of the individual person – a process of spiritual transformation which begins by evoking in them the kind of faith which draws them into an essentially mystical contact with the visionary dimensions of the religious mystery which surrounds and defines their experience of themselves as human beings. If Catholicism and its workings as a spiritual religion are to be understood – I am inclined to think it is easier to deal with it as a unique spirituality rather than as one religion among others – then it is on these deep and difficult foundations that an explanation needs to be based. All this leaves a great deal to be explained; but it is with the right kind of faith-experience that a start must be made.

❧

The faith-experience described in the Hebrews passage finds few echoes in the faith which is described in the source from which most modern adult Catholics have probably drawn their notion of it. Before it was indefinitely adjourned, the First Vatican Council (1869–70) worked under severe pressure from time and circumstance on two themes: to counter what it saw as the glorification of reason – 'rationalism' – by reaffirming the role of revelation and faith; and to provide clearly defined teaching about the Church itself. The latter issue was never adequately dealt with, and, to the alarm of many, all that was famously defined was the Petrine primacy and the infallibility of the Pope. But the Council had time to deal with faith and the relationship of human reason to it. It is worthwhile glancing briefly through the chapter 'On Faith', if only to see the sharp contrast between its view of faith and that of Hebrews above. (Latin text in Denzinger-

Schönmetzer, *Enchiridion Symbolorum*, ##3008-3014)

Vatican I's view of faith is of a supernatural virtue by which, with the help of God's grace, we believe that the things which have been revealed by God are true, not because we can appreciate their intrinsic truth by the natural light of our reason, but because of the authority of the infallible God who reveals them. As support for this view, the first sentence of the Hebrews passage is quoted (#3008). But then, in order to bring the compliance of our faith into agreement with reason – to make it 'reasonable' (*fidei nostrae obsequium rationi consentaneum*) – God has decided that to the internal aids of the Holy Spirit there should be joined 'divine deeds' (*facta ... divina*) as external arguments for his revelation. These are miracles and prophecies. In clearly manifesting God's omnipotence and infinite knowledge, they serve as signs of divine revelation which are entirely certain and well suited to the intelligence of all (#3009). The faith which leads to salvation requires the enlightenment and inspiration of the Holy Spirit. It is a gift of God whereby a man is freely obedient to God through willing cooperation with God's grace (#3010). Such an account of faith is worlds away from the faith-experience described in Hebrews, and obviously Vatican I, in the interests of a narrow theological correctness meant to fend off 'rationalist' error, is concentrating on a technically desiccated analysis of what was understood at that time by the interior act of faith which the Church demanded of Catholics. It is not giving an imaginatively enriched account of what is, or should be, involved in the experience of Catholic faith.

Following this technical analysis of faith, roughly summarized here, come four paragraphs (##3011–3014) which strongly emphasize the Church's supreme role in declaring what has been revealed and what must be believed 'by divine and catholic faith'. So dependent is our salvation on this faith that God founded the Church through his Son and marked it out publicly so that it could be recognised by everyone as 'the guardian and teacher of the revealed word'. In fact, the Church enjoys a monopoly (*ad solam ... Ecclesiam ea pertinent omnia*) over the many marvellous things which God has done to support the credibility of the Christian faith; and it is not too much to say that the Church itself, through its spread, its holiness, its ceaseless good works, its unity and its stability, represents 'a kind of great, permanent motive of credibility and an irrefutable proof' that it has been delegated by God for this task. The Church is a sign raised for the nations, leading men from darkness into light; and faithful Catholics can have no possible reason for changing or doubting their faith.

It is not difficult to see how these bold assertions, however triumphalistic or even somewhat paranoid as they may now sound, were intended to be a measured and thoughtful reaction to the problems which confronted the Church of that time. The Church's role in the matter of saving faith was vigorously exalted, and human reason (in the limited sense in which the Council understood it) was firmly relegated to its subordinate place. Reason played no part that was internal to faith, because all that was assigned to reason was the relatively simple task of reading the external signs which God, in his kindness, deigned to provide. In a way that seems almost uncomplimentary to God, human reason is treated like some backward child who has to be confronted with revealed truths which are beyond his grasp, and whose special educational needs are to be satisfied by the Church as his permanent tutor, if he is ever to grasp what he can of them – although, to be fair, in the following chapter on faith and reason (##3015–3020), a more positive role is assigned to reason. Not, of course, that reason can ever have direct knowledge of God's mysteries in the way it knows its own proper objects. But there cannot be a real disagreement (*vera dissensio*) between faith and reason, because it is the same God who reveals his mysteries and infuses faith, and who endows the human soul with the light of reason. Bogus disagreements arise particularly when the dogmas of faith are not understood and expounded 'according to the mind of the Church' (*ad mentem Ecclesiae*). But faith and reason can also be of some mutual assistance. 'Right reason' (*recta ratio*) displays the foundations of faith, and enlightened by faith it cultivates (*excolat*) the knowledge of divine matters (presumably a reference to theology), while faith frees and guards reason from errors, and furnishes it 'with much increased knowledge' (*multiplici cognitione*). Far be it from the Church to stand in the way of 'human arts and disciplines'. It promotes them, but they must stay within their proper territory. As far as dogmas are concerned, 'that meaning (*sensus*) which Holy Mother Church has declared once and for all must be retained for ever, and it must never be abandoned under the pretext or in the name of a higher understanding' (#3020).

It may seem strange to have dwelt on Vatican I at such length. I have done so for a number of reasons. First, I find it sad that the official documents of the Church, carefully composed by some of the most intelligent men of their generation, are now so little known. I daresay that what Vatican I says about faith has filtered down to most older Catholics, probably in some crudely garbled form; but there is no substitute for looking at the original texts. More often than not, it is only the negative and restrictive features of the Church's teachings that gain common currency; whereas I happen to think that much sound and positive theological sense is nearly always to be found in the texts, especially those issued by the greater Councils, including Vatican I. Secondly, it is crucial to realize how inevitably time-conditioned such documents are. What they say must always be understood in the light of the problems with which the Church thought itself confronted at a particular time. Vatican I took place almost a century and a half ago, and there can be no doubt that, for all Vatican I's insistence that certain matters were settled once and for all, nowadays a seriously defining Council might well express itself differently on the same theme of faith and reason. Disappointingly, Vatican II, pursuing a largely pastoral agenda through its many Constitutions, Decrees and Declarations, chose not to deal with faith in terms which differed substantially from the language of Vatican I; although 'the obedience of faith' to God's revelation is given a less theological, more personal twist, when it is described as 'an obedience by which man entrusts his whole self freely to God, offering "the full submission of intellect and will to God who reveals" [Vatican I], and freely assenting to the truth revealed by

Faith

Him' (*Dei Verbum*, On Divine Revelation, 18 November 1965, #5). But Vatican II's attitude is understandable. Any Council will want to think that certain matters have been settled by its predecessors for ever – that, for instance, no further understanding of the Church's dogmas once defined is required or possible. But not only have most Councils never in fact enjoyed much success with the reception of their conclusions, it is also obvious that trying to put a stop to further understanding is both impossible and counterproductive. The building of a dogmatic tradition has been an indispensable factor in the life of the Church; but such a tradition exists precisely because further human understanding has always required further interpretation and formulation. The history of ideas will not stop for anyone. Thirdly, as I said, I wanted to contrast the spiritual and imaginative experience of faith as viewed by Hebrews with the analysis of the theologically correct act of faith as viewed by Vatican I.

My reading of Vatican I is that, whilst the immediate circumstances made it necessary for the Church to call reason, in a rationalistic sense, to heel and to stress the authoritative role of the Church in the matter of faith, the Council could not bring itself to suppress human reason's role in faith altogether. To have done so would scarcely be a compliment to reason's Creator. But reason's input finds itself confined to an 'extrinsic' role. Any 'intrinsic' intelligibility that the divine mysteries have is God's alone. The distinction 'extrinsic-intrinsic' is typical of the Catholic apologetics of an earlier age. I can quite understand why it was used, since it serves to keep the workings of human reason in their place and at a safe distance; but at the cost, it seems to me, of denying to the faithful anything but the most indirect experience or contact with God's mystery, and then only in terms which are authorized by the Church. Reason is severely limited to reading the clues to God's mystery which it is for God to reveal, and for the Church to approve. But I am convinced that this last concession seriously understates the positive scope that the Council itself appears to leave open even to its own reduced view of reason. True, there are 'mysteries hidden away in God' (*mysteria in Deo abscon-*

dita) which are proposed to us for our belief, and which cannot be known unless God reveals them:

> But reason, enlightened by faith, provided it enquires diligently, piously and soberly, achieves, when God grants it, a measure of understanding of those mysteries – and a very productive one at that (*mysteriorum intelligentiam eamque fructuosissimam assequitur*). This it does both by analogy based on the things which it knows naturally, and on the connection which the mysteries themselves have with one another and with man's final end. (#3016)

So, supposing that the human reason works seriously and in the light of what faith contributes, and that it remains aware of the indirect, analogous or (as I would prefer to say) metaphorical nature of the knowledge of God's mysteries which it can garner from its connatural world or from reflecting on the nexus that exists between the mysteries themselves and between them and our human destiny – under such strict conditions it appears that the human reason can indeed strive to achieve some positive but 'slant' and indirect knowledge of the divine mysteries or mystery which transcend its capacities. 'The assent of faith' is 'in no way a blind movement of the mind' (*nequaquam ... motus animi caecus*, #3010). In its eloquently guarded way, the Council leaves open the possibility of a rational, imaginative, and surely also 'intrinsically' cognitive input into the experience and attitude of faith. This rather grudging concession on the Council's part licenses, I believe, the more positive understanding view of faith I intend to take.

The matter is far from unimportant. It is hard to think why God should, so to speak, begrudge his creatures access to his mysterious reality – the mystery wherein, when it is accepted and shared in faith, must lie our salvation. What kind of God are we dealing with here? Indeed, what sort of creatures must we suppose human beings are, if their Creator insists on holding them at arm's length, so to speak, from that contact with his own mystery which is the salvation of their humanity? Do Catholics believe in a God who would do this in the interests of the kind of superficial theological correctness which likes to pose as orthodoxy? An unacceptable gap is opened up between Creator and creature – a gap which, in the view of Vatican I, is bridgeable, of course, only through the intervention of the Church. It is possible to see Vatican I's general downgrading of the function of human reason in Catholic faith as part of a strategy which is meant to lead to an aggrandizement of the function of the Church in that faith. Not that I think the Church has no role to play in Catholic faith – far from it, as we shall see – but I cannot see that the Church's function is as 'intrinsic' as Vatican I would make it. Whatever the case, the act of faith as theologically analysed by Vatican I seems far from being the creative, constructive faith-experience described by Hebrews.

The reason for this, I am sure, is that Vatican I was in no position to give an adequate exposition of faith as long as it saw human powers such as reason as some kind of potential threat to faith. This led the Council, as I have said, to diminish reason's role in faith to a point where it was almost entirely subject to the Church's interpretation of what constituted Catholic faith, whilst not denying to reason some capacity for approaching the transcendent mystery of God under strictly limited and carefully monitored conditions. The Council lacked both the motive and the richer understanding of reason which might, in other circumstances, have enabled it to assign a larger role to the human mind and imagination in the act of faith.

Now the key factor which I think was lacking in its understanding of reason was an appreciation that essential to the full operation of reason is the functioning of the imagination, the faculty of forming mental images, the creative power of the rational mind itself. Given the human mind's constitutive dependence on the senses, the idea of 'pure reason' is, of course, a philosophical myth which has long had its day. At the time of Vatican I it was still highly influential and its claims had to be challenged. But in reality the human reason operates in a complex and 'impure' way on the basis of its own 'prejudices' – its prior understandings, its *Vorverständnisse* – and its imaginative insights, and mainly by the creative construction of metaphors and analogies to express the cognitive gains it manages to achieve in accordance with its variable ability. If this creative, constructive process is called for at the normal or natural level of understanding the world in which we live – as it certainly is – then it must also be called for all the more at the elevated level of understanding the mysteries involved in the sheer experience of existing as a human being. No doubt these mysteries, when they concern God, call for our religious faith, but it is a faith in which the rational imagination must have a key role to play. Religious faith, I would say, is a matter of personal, rational and imaginative insight into the mystery of God which surrounds and – if we are willing to let it – defines us as human beings. For a Catholic, the authoritative articulation and expression of the theological vision which the human imagination creates on the basis of its faith-experience is to be found in the Church's belief-system forged in the Church's doctrinal tradition. Between Catholic faith and Catholic beliefs there is a clear distinction, but also a strong co-inherence, interdependence and cooperation. To make the visionary experience of the mystery which we discern in our own humanity possible – the mystery we call God – faith and beliefs, I suggest, have to work together. It is this visionary experience, essentially mystical as it is, which merits the name of full and true Catholic faith.

※

With the re-introduction of the creative imagination into the experience of Catholic faith, we are brought back to its description in Hebrews. Faith is characteristic of people with a distinctly religious attitude towards their world. They detect, discern, a mystery about their experience of being human which they call their God. They put their faith in this mystery – commit themselves to it and entrust their lives to it and understand their lives in its light – and in turn the mystery they have discerned endows the hopes they have for themselves with reality, drawing the person with faith out of themselves into a state in which they are enabled to love the mystery which characterizes their own and, of course, everybody else's humanity. In other words, the mystery, accepted in faith, begins to work a transformation in them and in their world. They are increasingly enabled, through the gratuitous power (or 'grace') of the mystery they have discerned – or, as it may be expressed, in the 'Spirit' of that mystery – to view their whole world in the light of the mystery they call God. In such ways faith, drawn by the mystery called God, involves a constant and positive exercise of the religious imagination, a conscious and deliberate will to see the reality of the world, contrary appearances and experiences and other obstacles notwithstanding, as centred on the mystery of God. Subsumed in such faith are its attendant virtues of hope and love. Faith is a firm and trusting commitment to living and dying in terms of this essentially mystical attitude. Faith consists of a comprehensively spiritual 'take' on reality. It is no merely pious or theologically correct attitude; and it has nothing in common with baseless fantasy. It is a thoroughly down-to-earth, consciously chosen attitude, powered by the creative religious imagination, towards the experienced fact of one's own individual and personal existence, an attitude which claims to have its own kind of cognitive standing. '*Fides quaerit intellectum*' – faith seeks understanding, we usually say. But the translation is weak: *quaerit* can also mean 'demands', 'is out to get', understanding. Faith positively creates its own form of understanding, and insists on 'reading' or interpreting surrounding reality in the light of that mystery on which it rests, the mystery which humankind is invited, through serious reflection, to recognize and acknowledge, and which it can, in religious terms, only call its God. There are, of course, other terms in which other rationally imaginative projects or constructs invite us to understand our world in a certain way, including those which base themselves rigorously on empirical phenomena and are scientific in their method. But the phenomenon on which a religion like Catholicism bases itself is the experience of the mystery which is discerned as enveloping the very fact of being human; and insofar as it has a method – and the wrong method can be the death of it – it is a matter of the spiritual discipline which leads it to remain true to that experience.

I am speaking of faith in its broadest and most basic sense, because the kind of faith spoken about in Hebrews expressly involves hope, and as St Paul saw, love (or 'charity') as well. Paul realized that the interplay of faith, hope and love made them three aspects of a single response to the mystery of God which begins with faith, perseveres in hope and flowers as love:

> Therefore, since we are justified by *faith*, we have peace with God through our Lord Jesus Christ, through whom we have obtained access [by faith] to this grace in which we stand; and we boast in our *hope* of sharing the glory of God. And not only that, but we also boast in our sufferings, knowing that suffering produces endurance, and endurance produces character, and character produces *hope*, and *hope* does not disappoint us, because God's *love* has been poured into our hearts through the Holy Spirit that has been given to us.
> (Romans 5:1–5, my italics)

Or again:

> ... we have heard of your *faith* in Christ Jesus and of the *love* that you have for all the saints, because of the *hope* laid up for you in heaven. (Colossians 1:4–5, my italics)

In its masterly decree on justification, the Council of Trent (Session VI, 13 January 1547, Denzinger-Schönmetzer, ##1520–1583) picks up this text of Paul's and spells out the role which faith, hope and love together play in our salvation:

> ... the love of God is poured out through the Holy Spirit in the hearts of those who are being justified, and it becomes inherent (*inhaeret*) in them. Hence it is that in justification itself, through Jesus Christ into whom he is engrafted (*cui inseritur*), man has poured into him (*infusa accipit*) all these together: faith, hope and love (#1530).

This is because

> unless hope and love are added to it, faith neither unites [a person] perfectly with Christ, nor makes [a person] a living member of his body. For this reason it is most truly said that

'on its own faith is dead, unless it involves works' (cf. James 2:17 Greek) and is a waste of time (*otiosam*); and 'in Christ Jesus neither circumcision nor uncircumcision counts for anything; but [what counts] is faith which is rendered operative [*energoumenê*] through love'. (*Galatians* 5:6 Greek, #1531)

Catholic tradition refers to faith, hope and love as the theological virtues – 'virtues', in the sense that they work as interior spiritual powers or strengths of the person who possesses and practices them; and – rather quaintly – 'theological', in the sense that together they constitute the direct response we are enabled to make to the inviting demands of the mystery of God – the very mystery that enables and empowers those virtues in us. Hence they are also described as God's 'infused' gifts, given when we come to acknowledge that it is by a mystery which we can only count as divine that our humanity is enveloped and defined. Faith, hope and love are seen as God-inspired responses which take us – continually, mystically, even in a sense ecstatically – out of ourselves, and makes of us people who, despite the obstacles which time and life's fortunes and misfortunes place in our way, are prepared to keep faith with our own mystery, maintain the hopes we have of it, and exercise our love towards the world of our fellow humankind in which we continue to live our ordinary lives. The theological virtues draw us out of our sinful selves into a participation in that transcendent mystery where – with all the paradox that only a mystery can prompt – we come to find our better, saved selves 'in God'. Sometimes faith is likened to taking mindless 'leaps' – 'blind faith', 'leaps of faith' towards some nameless Beyond. Less is said about 'leaps of hope' or 'leaps of love', though hope and love, no less than the faith with which they are allied, also depend on our being prepared to take the spiritual risk of living by the vision of a reality which is centred on the transcendent mystery of God which we see as defining and characterizing our humanity. What takes us out of ourselves is the dynamic openness or power of self-transcendence which all three mutually conditioning theological virtues have. Faith bespeaks vision, hope fulfilment, love union – all indicating directions in which we are meant to be growing through their exercise. In their way, they already anticipate, proleptically, future growth and development. How faith, hope and love may be thought to correlate closely with the serious experience of being human will be suggested later.

In passing I might mention that the idea of self-transcendence, which we have associated with the theological virtues that form part of the Catholic doctrinal tradition, has enjoyed a more secular usage, specifically as the antidote to what is called alienation, the pathological self-estrangement whereby persons refuse to become themselves or to involve themselves in reality. It is as if human beings are faced with a simple choice: either they have constantly to transcend themselves by reaching out beyond themselves into what their own mystery enables and requires them to achieve, or they succumb to withering into a state of alienation, a refusal to be what they are truly meant to become. This is not a field of study where I feel at home; but I offer the following remarks of the remarkable Canadian Jesuit philosopher, Bernard Lonergan, in support of this view.

> The term, alienation, is used in many different senses. But on the present analysis the basic form of alienation is man's disregard of the transcendental precepts, Be attentive, Be intelligent, Be reasonable, Be responsible ... As self-transcendence promotes progress, so the refusal of self-transcendence turns progress into terminal decline. Finally we may note that a religion that promotes self-transcendence to the point, not merely of justice, but of self-sacrificing love, will have a redemptive role in human society inasmuch as such love can undo the mischief of decline and restore the cumulative process of progress. (*Method in Theology*, p. 55)

Lonergan's insight belongs to a perspective different from mine, but it confirms the need for the constant stretching out of the self – for him into the exercise of the powers of the mind, for me into the exercise of the theological virtues of faith, hope and love – in order to achieve the progress and personal growth which alone will make us who we really are.

If my view of faith, with attendant hope and active love, has made these three virtues basic to what is strictly a

Faith

mystical and self-transcending stance in the face of the world – a measure of participation in the mystery of being human which we can only call God – then I shall have laid what I think is the proper foundation for an understanding of Catholicism and of how it works. Despite the strictly analytical treatment accorded the theologically correct act of faith in the Church's later tradition, the experience of faith, along with the ways we experience hope and love, are no abstract, disembodied attitudes recommended by Church authority to be struck by those who wish to live pious and blameless lives, and die holy deaths. They spring from and embody imaginative insights into the human condition which lead us into personal encounters with what we can – mysteriously but truly – only call divine about ourselves: our God-assisted ability to cope with the necessities, the demands, which being human among other humans lays upon us; and thereby to live our ordinary lives in ways that begin to overcome and heal our innate limitations and deficiencies. Catholicism, I believe, is a religion – better, at root a mystical or visionary spirituality – which is precisely meant to enable us to do this. How all this might be true, and how it might work, is what I have taken upon myself to expound. We must begin with faith and its associated virtues, which in Catholicism bespeak a mystical attitude towards the world. This attitude results from what is known as *metanoia* – conversion from an old mind-set to a new one. A whole new imaginative interpretation is put on being human in the world, in response to the mystery of being human which we call God.

※

But for all that I have tried to describe the imaginative character of faith, that character will remain irritatingly vague and disembodied until it is actually discovered at work in the life of a person of faith. The human attitude of faith is not revealed to, or visited on, humankind from some outside source, abstractly, extrinsically; because, as I have been suggesting, it is an attitude which it belongs to our human potential to receive and assume, and which actualizes that potential when freely adopted as the properly human response to the invitation to a spiritually transformed life offered by humanity's own mystery which we call God. As far as Catholicism is concerned, the individual person to whom the fundamental faith-insight was first vouchsafed was Abraham, 'our father in faith'. Abram (as he then was) was inspired to leave his small, familiar world behind, and to head for the imaginative horizons of new meaning that were being promised him:

> Now the Lord said to Abram, 'Go from your country and your kindred and your father's house to the land that I will show you. I will make of you a great nation, and I will bless you, and make your name great, so that you will be a blessing. I will bless those who bless you, and the one who curses you I will curse; and in you all the families of the earth shall be blessed.' (Genesis 12.1–3)

Contained in this foundational tale are the elements of what should be meant by religious faith in the Catholic tradition. Abraham's faith consisted in his willingness to move beyond his own tame, literal world and to adopt and share in the imaginative vision which was being promised to him and his descendants. It is a paradigm of the dynamic experience of faith – a paradigm that was fleshed out in the development of the religion of the chosen people of Israel through the insights of Moses and the other prophets, and in the growth of Jewish religious cult and law. Behind all this lay the inspiration derived from Abraham's original insight, and eventually it was the characteristic vision of the world which Judaism had constructed which provided the religious setting which was native to Jesus. Further, it was within the religious tradition of Judaism that Jesus' own radically fresh religious insight into reality occurred, and that a new vision of reality was constructed. Its construction involved a dangerously new departure from what had become the domesticated religious norm. Only such a supposition will explain the hostility which Jesus appears to have aroused in his co-religionists. In the span of his brief public ministry, Jesus was intent on offering a vivid reinterpretation of Judaism which was judged by the Jewish religious authorities radically heterodox enough to threaten their central religious tradition and to make them call for the death penalty.

The early preaching of the Christian Gospel, and not least the gospel accounts of Jesus' passion and death, however they may have inevitably over-polarized the differences between Jesus and contemporary Judaism, leave little room for doubt that Jesus was reacting in a conscious, deliberate and authoritative fashion against his co-religionists. He was, in his way, something of a heretic. He felt himself positively empowered to choose his own religious position (which is what *hairesis* came to mean in Greek), and to put his own personal interpretation on the foundational faith-attitude of Abraham, setting it against the traditional interpretations of Judaism: 'Your ancestor Abraham rejoiced that he would see my day; he saw it and was glad ... Very truly, I tell you, before Abraham was, I am' (John 8:56, 58). His religious insight (whatever its source) retained a rooted continuity with Abraham and Judaism, but reinterpreted its meaning: 'You have heard that it was said ... But I say to you ...' (Matthew 5:21). He was seeking to replace the traditional construction which Judaism had put on the faith-attitude of Abraham with a new interpretation based on insights of a new intensity which came from his own personal faith. It is to the faith of Jesus and to what it is meant to entail that, in their widely different ways, the New Testament writings testify.

⁂

Catholic theology has consistently shied away from considering the human faith of Jesus as a factor which has any part to play in the theologically correct understanding of him. The accepted orthodoxy has virtually ruled out the idea that Jesus could have possessed ordinary human faith. The reason behind this astonishingly improbable position has usually been that human faith in Jesus would have been incompatible with what is theologically called his personal divinity. If he was God, why would he need faith? To endow Jesus, even to associate him, with human faith was seen as tantamount to a denial of his divinity. Obviously there will be more to be said later about the Catholic dogmatic mentality and its suppositions about the nature of divinity and humanity, both of which are no doubt rightly predicated of Jesus from the technically correct doctrinal point of view. But for the moment it must be enough to say that the refusal to ascribe ordinary human faith to Jesus in the interests of maintaining his divinity is, of course, tantamount to a denial of his full and perfect humanity – a factor without which Jesus would, at a stroke, be completely disqualified as the Saviour of humankind in any Catholic sense. Early theologians, far more keenly aware of the implications of theology for the real processes of salvation than later generations, realized that it was essential to our salvation that Jesus was fully human when they condemned docetic views, according to which Jesus' humanity was no more than an unreal appearance, as well as the fuller blown fourth-century heresy of Apollinarius, who declared Jesus' whole human psychology surplus to the requirements of his personal divinity, and actually saw in it a factor whose necessary presence in a real humanity would disrupt the perfect union of God with man. In any case, what possible use could Jesus have for a human mind if he was God's Word incarnate?

This whole problem with the faith of Jesus and its supposed incompatibility with his divinity is, of course, an example of how a theological requirement – Jesus' divinity – can be understood in a way which creates a problem which, as far as we can tell from an intelligent reading of the Gospels, simply did not exist. The theological tail is encouraged to wag the religious dog. Jesus' 'divinity' is being considered literally as a separable item in his total make-up, and that creates a fake problem for that other separable item in his make-up, his 'humanity'. But uncreated and infinite 'divinity' could never be an item comparable with other created and finite items, so that a clash is created when they are brought together. We cannot know, in any case, what is meant by 'divinity', or why it must exclude human faith. Is 'divinity' to be thought of as antithetical to humanity? In which case how is humanity to be saved by the divine? Or how can divinity's perfect revelation be a human being? All we can say is what we know of our own humanity – a

Faith

humanity identical with that of Jesus – namely that faith is a characteristic of humanity, so that whatever 'divinity' means, it is not incompatible with it. The all-too-common problem with Jesus' human faith is a theologically manufactured piece of nonsense. I cannot recall anyone supposing that Jesus had no human hope or no human love. Yet if it is the case, as I have said, that hope and love along with faith have to do with how we can best cope with our experience of human existence as such, it is unimaginable that Jesus, who certainly experienced human existence to the full in his life and in the suffering which led to his death, could have lacked any of these key human virtues.

※

The effective strategy against being waylaid by such bogus theological problems must be a return to the religious faith which must surely be normative for Catholicism – the human faith of Jesus himself. This is not the place to display the detailed findings of a lengthy trawl through the New Testament evidence which bears on Jesus as the normative man of faith, if only because there is a surprising amount of it, both in St Paul's letters, where it is often lost in translation, and of course in the Gospels. Nor is this the place for me to pretend to a technical expertise in biblical studies which I do not possess, though I would say I was very familiar with the New Testament, and especially with its style of Greek. In any case experience has shown that it is not to be expected that a detailed argument would be readily accepted by professional biblical scholars or theologians who often seem bent on protecting their own hard-won expertise. Behind such naive expectations lies the mistake of supposing that it is ever easy to achieve a single agreed and standard interpretation of textual data in any field of study, let alone in biblical studies where a prior commitment to some predetermined interpretation is perhaps especially likely to make its presence felt. In exegesis, as in other human disciplines, it seems that progress can best be made dialectically – by discussion between opposing theories rather than by the forced exclusion of any one of them. There is, of course, an irreducibly subjective element in any kind of reading, whether of texts or of other products of human artistry, and individuals will always 'read' what is in front of them against a background either of personal experience or of some acquired intellectual or spiritual 'horizon'. Even a deliberate and sustained effort to be completely 'objective' would presumably be based, if only unconsciously, on some sort of pre-adopted theory. 'Prejudice' in the technical sense – prior understanding, *Vorverständnis* – is simply a fact of intellectual life. I freely admit that this is the case with my own 'reading' of the New Testament as a collection of texts which I find have much more to say about the human faith of Jesus than is generally supposed, as well as preaching a gospel of salvation which is far more dependent on that faith than people are prepared to imagine.

The human faith of Jesus embodies the characteristic attitude he showed towards his own experience of human existence in the process of being born, living, working and dying as part of humankind. It would be obviously wrong, as I have said, to deprive Jesus of just the kind of human mind and imagination which we all have; and equally wrong to suppose that he did not use his human mind and imagination to try to interpret and understand, on the basis of his own human experience, what sense human life made, and how best it might be approached and managed. There is nothing human that is alien to Jesus. The doctrinal claim that Jesus was divine does nothing whatever to diminish or alter the integrity of his humanity. Indeed, as we shall see, in the dogmatic thinking of the Church, his divinity renders his humanity paradigmatically more, and certainly not less, human than our own (Cf. *The Chalcedonian Definition*, Denzinger-Schönmetzer, #302 – and see below). So we should have no hesitation in attributing to Jesus all the intelligence, thoughtfulness, powerful emotions, humour, close sympathies, sensitivity, courage and, especially in his teaching, the creative imagination which we find abundantly evidenced in the Gospels – and not as the by-products or side-effects of some divine factor in which we cannot share, but as belonging to an outstanding humanity which he shares fully with ourselves.

In its centuries-long concern with dogmatic correctitude, Catholicism has certainly run the risk of letting the divinity of Jesus override his undoubted humanity; and, as a result, it has been possible to discern in Catholics a lack of a down-to-earth sense of Jesus' humanity. Even all my talk about Jesus the man rather than about the dogmatically defined Christ may strike older Catholics as suspect. Compensation for this deficiency has to some extent been found in the development in Catholicism of various thoroughly sensible 'devotions' – for instance, to the Sacred Heart of Jesus and to his Mother, and also to those often notable examples of humanity, the saints. Whilst such devotions remain entirely praiseworthy in themselves, they can be seen as indications of a need for an appreciation of Jesus' and others' humanity in Catholicism which, strictly speaking, should have been satisfied by a soundly orthodox official understanding of the full and real humanity of Jesus himself. It was this understanding that was among the very first to emerge from the vigorous opposition to the Gnostic heresies mounted by the earliest theologians. That it took some four centuries before it was definitively established is some indication of how powerful the temptation to assert the divinity of Jesus at the expense of his humanity, and vice versa, has been. Not, of course, that the full and real humanity of Jesus can be simply a matter of theological debate. On Jesus' humanity, as the earliest theologians realized, hinges the very possibility of Catholic salvation.

Given, then, a Jesus who even in theological terms was as human as the rest of us, we can safely assume that he confronted the reality of being human and the human world as we all have to do, and approached it through much the same exercise of our common human faculties. The vital difference between him and us lies in the authority with which he personally made a radically new attitude towards humanity his own. From the gospel accounts it appears that after spending most of his life in obscurity, he reached a point at which, for one reason or another, he found himself able to adopt a new personal insight into his own experience of being human – an insight which he then began to interpret and understand with authority, and to build into a new religious vision through the power of his own mind and his creative imagination. He discovered that the new interpretation and understanding of his own humanity required, not surprisingly, that he should draw on the contemporary religion of his native Judaism for its theological articulation. There was no other obvious source of ideas and terms for Jesus to use, and his use of it caused the deepening tensions with his co-religionists which eventually led to his death. It was not that Jesus, as he said, set out to scrap Judaism: 'Do not think that I have come to abolish the law or the prophets; I have come not to abolish but to fulfil' (Matthew 5:17). But his use of Jewish materials for the expression of his new visionary insight into his own humanity strained those materials to breaking point: 'No one sews a piece of unshrunk cloth on an old cloak, for the patch pulls away from the cloak, and a worse tear is made …' (Matthew 9:16).

Such words not only define the position Jesus was taking with regard to Judaism, but, if they are anything like authentic, also display something of his colourful, almost breezy personal style. Far from simply recycling the religious truths he had learnt from Judaism – truths to do with the Kingdom or the Fatherhood of God – he was publicly re-interpreting them, giving them a new meaning which the traditional terms would not accommodate. He was proposing a radically new theology. He was re-imagining God in the light of his new understanding of his experience of being human. It is extremely difficult for Catholics who have learned to view Jesus chiefly through the thick smoke and distorting mirrors of theological controversy, in the bland products of religious portraiture, or through so much heavily stained glass, to recapture something of the courageous flair and freshness of a man possessed of a vivid new insight into his own experience of being human, an insight which was demanding to be preached and taught to disciples, to be built into a transmissible spiritual vision which would lead to the radical transformation of what it meant to be human. Here was a man of supremely creative imagination with a gift for metaphor and parable and with little time to lose, up against a religion which he had found to be obscuring or deadening what he considered to be the mysterious truth about being human instead of bringing it to life and revealing the real dimensions of humankind. Far better than any ancient or modern biography could possibly have done, the Gospels create a new literary genre which succeeds in catching the feel of the pressures which Jesus' experience of being human imposed on him, along with his reactions to them, and not least towards what was to be the end of his brief life. In the Gospels we sense the sudden upsurge of his new insight and vision after what proves to be almost a lifetime of preparation followed by a shock confrontation with the new truth in what was becoming a personal desert. Importantly, we also hear of his occasional doubts, still troubling him at the end in the garden from which he was taken to suffer, and on the Cross where he was to die; of his warm sympathy with his fellow human beings in their physical and spiritual needs; of his attractive brilliance as a teacher; his authority as a leader; the driven urgency of what he saw as his saving mission; of his hostility towards those who would obstruct that mission; of his search for reliable and understanding disciples; of his relationships with his family and his friends. What the Gospels are doing, in their way, is giving an account of a man possessed of a radically new insight into his own humanity and into that of his fellow human beings, an account of a man with a new theological vision which he has fashioned, with all the power of his own creative imagination, out of the elements of a moribund Judaism, a new man, a new Adam, a new Abraham, a man of hope, of love, and especially of faith.

Familiarity – or ignorance – can easily lead us to forget the strangeness, the uniqueness of the Gospels. Their oddity rests on the fact that they are the products of an unfamiliar kind of theology – a theology of Jesus whose real starting-point, notwithstanding the understandable embellishments that were attached to them, is not his divinity but his humanity. Or rather, theologies of Jesus: since each Gospel, and most transparently the fourth, has its own theological 'take' on Jesus. Not that the Gospels were the first attempts to render a theological account of Jesus. In his letters Paul, beset by problems and controversies in the pagan cities where he had contact with nascent Christian communities, had contrived to give a theological account of Jesus which was more intellectual, more technical, and more abstract. This was the kind of account, we can suppose, that would appeal to, or at least impress, Paul's varied audiences. In an environment where the dominant religions centred on a plurality of pagan gods, it was natural that Paul would stress the intimate association of Jesus with the unique divinity of the Father and his Spirit. It is often alleged that the humanity of Jesus plays little or no part in Paul's message. In fact, Paul, who had never met Jesus, even seems to consider Jesus' humanity irrelevant: 'So as from now we do not regard anybody in physical terms (*kata sarka*); even supposing that we had known Christ in physical terms, that is no longer the way we know him.' (2 Corinthians 5:16, my translation). But to suppose that Jesus' humanity was not important for Paul may well be to fail to see the religious wood for the theological trees – to ignore the fact that Paul makes much more religious capital out of the human faith of Jesus than is usually allowed.

This is a matter which calls for a much longer and more technical discussion than I can offer here. The distinction which Paul often makes between the law and faith is sufficiently well known. Paul held that as a vehicle of salvation the Jewish law has been replaced by faith. To take a fairly typical passage:

> Now before faith came, we were imprisoned and guarded under the law until faith would be revealed. Therefore the law was our disciplinarian until Christ came, so that we might be justified by faith. But now that faith has come, we are no longer subject to a disciplinarian, [v. 26] for in Christ Jesus you are all children of God through faith. As many of you as were baptized into Christ have clothed yourselves with Christ. There is no longer Jew or Greek, there is no longer slave or free, there is no longer male and female; for all of you are one in Christ Jesus. And if you belong to Christ, then you are Abraham's offspring, heirs according to the promise. (Galatians 3:23–29)

No discerning reader can avoid seeing the central importance of what is called 'faith' in this passage. It is faith which is salvifically operative throughout, and in multiple ways. Faith releases us from the hold which the law had over us; faith makes us children of God; through baptism faith 'clothes' us in Christ; faith overrides all racial, social and even gender distinctions; faith unites us all in Christ; faith establishes us as legitimate descendants and heirs of the original promise God made to Abraham because of his faith.

But there is a question about faith which is not generally asked – *whose* faith does all this? Supposing that faith is not meant to be taken, like 'the Law', as some abstract or personified principle of salvation – in which case it would become very difficult to see how it might actually bring about such remarkable effects – *whose* faith is in question here? Surely not our own faith, at least in the first instance. So *whose* faith in the first instance? It can only be the human faith of Jesus himself. It is my view that this faith is what Paul often writes about; and although he may have had little interest in the historical character of Jesus, he showed far more religious and spiritual interest in the humanity and the basic human qualities of Jesus than is sometimes asserted – and not least, of course, in his actual crucifixion. I think this point can be briefly reinforced by two textual arguments drawn from this section of Galatians – to which others could certainly be added.

I would translate verse 26, numbered in the above passage, straightforwardly as: 'for all of you are God's sons through the faith which is in Christ Jesus'. The NRSV translates it: 'for in Christ Jesus you are all children of God through faith'. The order of the Greek sentence has been – for what reason? – virtually reversed. I would accept that this might seem a rather foolishly trivial point to make, if it did not happen repeatedly in translations of Paul's letters that we find that our faith *in* Jesus Christ (that is, Jesus Christ as the *object* of our faith) has supplanted the faith *of* Jesus Christ (that is, Jesus Christ as the *subject* whose faith is meant). It might be thought that I have a theological bee in my religious bonnet about the faith of Jesus, and that I wish to ensure that in the letters of Paul, as in the Gospels, Jesus is always seen as the man of faith, the man whose faith, that is, constitutes the operative principle of our salvation. I do not think the textual evidence would support that unflattering judgement even after careful and lengthy argument. All I am saying is that there is more evidence for my view in Paul's letters than translators allow to meet the eye. For one thing, in Greek there is no discernible textual difference whatever between what is called an objective and a subjective genitive, and I would simply say that a subjective genitive usually gives a more natural and less strained translation than an objective one. Interestingly, and very properly, in the same section of Galatians, the NRSV translates 3:22 as: 'But the scripture has imprisoned all things under the power of sin, so that what was promised through faith in Jesus Christ [objective genitive] might be given to those who believe.' It then gives as an alternative translation of the phrase: 'Or "through the faith of Jesus Christ" [subjective genitive]'. An even stricter translation might run: 'in order that the promise which comes as result of Jesus Christ's faith might be passed on to those who have [that] faith.'

Obviously there is considerable room for lengthy discussion here, and I have mentioned only a couple of texts from many. But I do not wish to be further distracted from what I want to say: that despite Paul's lack of acquaintance with the human Jesus, Jesus' humanity, and particularly his human faith, plays a more substantial part in Paul's religion than is often thought. It seems that it is the faith of Jesus which makes the connections between several aspects of the mystical vision which inspired Paul's mission:

> I have been crucified with Christ; and it is no longer I who live, but it is Christ who lives in me. And the life I now live in the flesh I live by faith in the Son of God [the Greek has: 'I live in a faith which is that of the Son of God' – and the NRSV rightly gives the alternative: 'by the faith in the Son of God'] who loved me and gave himself for me. (Galatians 2:19–20)

It is by sharing in the faith of Jesus which came to its fullest and most loving expression in his sacrificial death in crucifixion on Calvary that Paul sees that we come to share in the salvation that Jesus has to offer. Through sharing in Jesus' faith we also come to share in his hope and in his love. Further, we come to share in Jesus' whole mystical vision of reality, the vision which inspired the way in which he had learned from his experience of being human how best to cope with the necessities, the demands, the imperatives, which human existence laid upon him.

> Let this same mind-set be in you [*touto phroneite*] that was also in Christ Jesus ... (Philippians 2:5, 'my translation')

❦

I suppose that it is often thought that Paul's interpretation of Jesus is more developed than that of the Gospels: that it is more intellectual, more sophisticated, wider in its ethnic appeal. Whilst this may be true, it must be recalled that, despite the familiar order of the books in the New Testament, Paul's Christology – his theological account of Jesus and his salvific function – is generally earlier than that of the written Gospels, though hardly earlier than the understanding of Jesus which inspired the materials from which the Gospels were eventually compiled. Paul's Christology is the highly personal construct of a theologically brilliant and deeply mystical religious mind driven by a convert's zeal. But during the period in which Paul was constructing his interpretation of Jesus, a tradition of different interpretations was forming in a number of different Christian centres. These interpretations, obviously dependent on one another in various complex ways, eventually settled down into the four Gospels as we know them, and without losing their distinctive characters.

It is fair to ask why, over the lengthy period of their development, they did not take on more of the intellectual and abstract quality of Pauline theological interpretation, but stuck to what we might think are the homelier forms of narrative, framing their interpretations of Jesus in more or less coherently narrative accounts of his life, work, death and resurrection. I think the answer must lie in the fact that, far from eschewing theological sophistication, they were subtly developing a quite different, possibly unique and perhaps even higher, form of theology. In its interpretation and understanding of Jesus this new form of theology did not seek to present him directly in the colourful and universal religious language which Paul found helpful in preaching his 'Christ Jesus'. Rather, the Gospels took what might be called a humanly 'embedded' approach to the way they wished Jesus to be understood. Their theological interpretation of Jesus would be found in the significant events which were considered to have made up his human life – his birth, his emergence from obscurity, his preaching, his miracles, his tours of Palestine, his gathering of disciples, his teaching of them, the growing opposition to him from Judaism. his final, fateful journey to Jerusalem, his suffering and death and unexpected resurrection. The accounts of these events are, of course, theologically loaded and tailored to make the desired impression. Jesus himself is endowed with roles and titles which express his authentic place as a definitive interpreter of the Jewish tradition. But the theology, the imaginative interpretation of Jesus' meaning, does not draw on the same religious world as does Paul – it stays firmly embedded in the significant matrix of his human life. This makes the Gospels a highly successful and sophisticated set of examples, newly invented for the purpose, of a theology of Jesus' true and full humanity. Some might be inclined to call it 'concrete', as opposed to abstract, theology. Whatever it may be called, it rests on the conviction that it is on Jesus' humanity that our salvation depends.

But not, I would want to insist, on his humanity as any kind of abstraction. What is crucial 'for us and for our salvation' is that he was a human being, and a human being who is the unique archetype and model of Abrahamic faith. Due consideration will be given to his divinity below. Hardly surprisingly, Jesus' divinity is a totally – better, infinitely – different issue from that of his humanity. We are not dealing with two comparable commodities or qualities, and it is better to treat them apart before trying to say how they might, in Catholic terms, be thought to be related to one another. If, as I have suggested, the theology of the Gospels is a theology of Jesus the man of faith, I might be expected to prove this by chapter and verse. I am of the opinion that this could certainly be done, but it would be a laborious and perhaps unnecessary process. The gospel evidence relevant to faith is, in my view, abundant and varied. All the same, this view depends on the openness of the attention with which a 'reading' of the Gospels is conducted. For instance, it would be necessary to be especially sensitive to the prominence of the verb 'to have faith' (*pisteuein*), with over 120 occurrences over all four Gospels, and over 70% of them in the Gospel of John. Not, of course, that each occurrence carries the same meaning or would have the same christological relevance. So all would have to be individually assessed and discussed. Or again, another approach to Jesus' faith would be to take the evident interest in Abraham himself, which should certainly be adduced as bearing on Jesus as the man of faith. Abraham is mentioned over thirty times in all four Gospels (though only once in Mark). Roughly two-thirds of this number could have some bearing, more or less direct, on the interpretation and understanding of Jesus. And there are other words, sayings, incidents and so forth that would have to be examined. But I find a more convincing case for Jesus as the man of faith can be made by basing it, not on text crunching, but on an appreciation of the thrust and purpose of the Gospels as such.

The Gospels, I am suggesting, represent a new genre of theology whose thrust and purpose is to preach a Jesus with a distinctive and characteristic new attitude towards the reality of humankind and the human world – an attitude which is comprehensively called his faith. His faith was what Jesus urgently invited others to share, because his experience of his own humanity, and of the mystery which surrounds the experience of human existence – the mystery he insisted on calling 'Father' – had convinced him that it was precisely in sharing his new religious faith and the new vision of reality it contained – the 'Kingdom of God' – that people would be saved. He was a man with a saving mission and a saving message. It was a message that he had developed from his own personal human insight into his own experience of being human. This experience he had interpreted and come to understand through a use of his own mind and imagination which could only strike people as a new and uniquely inspired revelation of God. Once the insight had been articulated into the message, and he was ready to preach it, for a year or two of intense activity it poured out of him in a confident stream of public teachings, parables, demonstrations of healing power, the private instruction of disciples, both men and women, until such time as public opposition both to him and to a message which could only sound subversive of the Judaism in the midst of which he worked, brought him to what seemed a disastrous end in the ignominy of a criminal's death by crucifixion.

To give his revealing insight into the mystery of humankind intelligent articulation, and to construct the new theological vision that went with it, Jesus naturally drew on the religious categories of his native Judaism. The resulting adaptation and reinterpretation of what were the cherished religious expressions of his fellow-Jews not only bred confrontation with them, but radically altered the meaning of those categories and expressions. What had, in Jesus' view, become dead religious metaphors which were being used to support moribund religious practices, had to be revived and re-used – in fact, re-metaphorized or re-mythologized – and put to new uses which would release the new meanings that they were needed to carry. The process can be detected in Jesus' radical recycling of certain 'titles' which were traditionally used of hoped-for leaders or representatives of the Jewish people – the Messiah or the Prophet or the Son of Man, for example. It appears that it was with the last title alone that Jesus felt at all comfortable, and only then when it denoted a representatively human figure with whom he could meaningfully identify. Similarly with Jesus' personal reinterpretation of 'the Kingdom of God'. But most tellingly, surely, with his radical reconstruction of the metaphor around which the religion of Judaism revolved – the name of 'God'. Jesus gave 'God' a new meaning. The name we have to give what we discern to be the transcendent mystery of our own humanity has the status of a metaphor. Jesus re-metaphorized the metaphor of 'God' into his personal metaphor of 'Father'. In so doing, he bypassed a whole religion based on the old metaphor, without destroying it, and founded a new religion centred on his own new metaphor. Jesus is not just toying with figures of speech. He was radically re-imagining 'God'. In doing this he was expressing new insight into his own humanity and its transcendent mystery, shifting the whole world of humanity into a new understanding of itself and its place in the world, and offering humankind a way of salvation from the frustrations and failures it faced when confronted with the demands that were revealed in reflection on the experience of existing as a human being.

I would say that the way salvation works for humankind in the Catholic tradition can only be through sharing the spirit of faith of Jesus, along with his hope and his love – sharing his inspired and inspiring insight into the mystery inherent in humanity, and sharing his vision of a world where God is called the Father who personally regards humankind as much his sons and heirs as Jesus himself, who inspires them with the same Spirit which binds Jesus the man of faith in Sonship with the Father. That such was the shape and the content of his followers' attachment to Jesus may be the truth which Paul summarized as follows:

> But when the fullness of time had come, God sent his Son, born of a woman, born under the law, in order to redeem those who were under the law, so that we might receive adoption as sons. And because you are sons, God has sent the Spirit of his Son into our hearts, crying 'Abba! Father!' So you are no longer a slave but a son, and if a son then also an heir, through God' [or 'an heir of God through Christ'].
> (Galatians 4:4–7 – I have replaced 'children/child' in the NRSV translation with sons/son, for the sake of theological clarity)

There is at the heart of Catholicism that indispensable element of mysticism which I have already noted, and it is this mystical union – a union in faith, hope and love – which led Paul to speak elsewhere in terms of such intensity about the Christian's relationship to Christ: about being baptized into Christ, clothed in Christ, being alive with a Christ who is within oneself. On the basis of a shared faith with Jesus there exists a spiritual and mutual mystical co-inherence of Christ and his followers, and it is this above all else that effects our necessary salvation. It is this that Catholicism has sought to keep as the foundation and core of the salvation it continues to offer. There is a deep form of Christocentric mysticism which lies at the heart of Catholicism, and without it Catholic salvation is ineffective. The rest of Catholicism (beliefs, creeds, doctrines, Church, sacraments, devotions, etc.) has been developed in order to articulate and support this core Catholic truth.

Chapter 3

Theologoumena

It may seem that the dominant role I have suggested for faith, as the religious response to the basic experience of our existence as human beings, and as the operative factor in our understanding of how Jesus is our Saviour, has so far been rather hard on Catholic theology. I have, for instance, contrasted the richly imaginative experience of faith as evidenced in Hebrews, and in the Jesus of the Gospels, with the barren, theologically correct analysis of the act of faith proposed by Vatican I. In all this theology may seem to have emerged as the loser, as a regrettably technical impediment to the properly religious understanding of the matter in hand. In fact, this is very far from being the truth as I see it; and I now wish to redress any imbalance that may have suggested itself. If there is one thing that can be fearlessly asserted in theology's favour, it is that Catholicism, as a working spiritual religion, would be lost without it. This is because without some form of theologically expressed response it would be humanly impossible to cope, however inadequately it may be, with the faith-experience of the mystery of our humanity – to think coherently about it, to speak intelligently about it, to preach and transmit it effectively, and even (I would say) to have the religious experience of mystery in the first place. Mystical experience, if it is to be at least in some measure transmissible, needs to be rendered articulate, to be articulated; and it is the chief purpose of the theological 'articles' of the Catholic belief-system to do precisely this. Theology is required to do proper justice to faith.

'Theologoumena' (the plural of 'theologoumenon') is an unusual word which ought to have a far wider currency than it has, if only because it is impossible to enter into a serious discussion about the meaning of Catholicism and its traditional doctrines without it. Theologoumena are statements or positions or conclusions arrived at and formulated by theologians as they pursue the craft of theology. Some theologoumena may remain nothing more significant than the personal opinions of one or a number of theologians. Others may achieve a wider currency among groups of followers within the Catholic doctrinal tradition. Others may be given the approval of ecclesiastical authority and be reckoned authentic expressions of the meaning and truth of the tradition. Others may be defined as parts, or 'articles', of Catholic teaching, and find themselves embedded in creeds or the decrees of councils or official catechisms. As such they become Catholic doctrines or dogmas, and Church authority requires them to be believed by the faithful. But at none of these rising levels of approval do the statements involved become detached from their roots in the minds and imaginations of the theologians who originally proposed them. However high their status in the hierarchy of Church approval, as linguistic artefacts – which is how I shall consider them – they remain ineradicably earth-bound theologoumena.

Not that this fact licenses their being taken lightly. On the contrary: thoroughly human contributions though they may be to Catholicism's doctrinal tradition, they still represent the ways in which Catholicism has contrived to understand itself over the centuries. But even the most solemn theologoumena now enshrined in the Catholic tradition remain open to the kind of scrutiny that any responsible use of human language may be called on to undergo. There is nothing linguistically sacrosanct about them, and it is no act of sacrilege to demand, with respect, what they might be meant to mean. I say all this in case anyone should think that my attitude to doctrinal statements is cavalier, or that I am treading unawares on ground where angels might fear to tread. But it is all very well for angels. Angels are not earth-bound Catholics.

They have, supposedly, no need for the kind of faith, allied with hope and love, which Catholics need, since the vision they are said to enjoy of the mystery we have to address as 'God' is more direct and immediate that ours. Nor, since they have no need of our kind of faith, do they have any need of our kind of system of beliefs to support it. Nor, since they are already spirits, do they need our form of spiritual religion. But I am writing about Catholics and their Catholicism – and they do need their faith, hope and love, and their system of beliefs to support them, as well as the spirituality which, I shall maintain, is what their Catholicism, properly understood, should provide for all. But properly understanding their Catholicism as the spirituality they need for the living of a human life and the dying of a human death involves understanding the particular form of faith, hope and love which form the heart of Catholicism, as well as understanding the nature and function of the religious beliefs and teachings which Catholics are called on to accept. Reaching this understanding of Catholicism involves mentally dismantling its spiritual workings and seeing how its various parts are meant to function, and looking honestly at the religious beliefs of Catholicism as theologoumena.

Perhaps nothing is commonly considered more characteristic of Catholicism than the system of religious beliefs – the theologoumena – which it requires its adherents to accept. Catholicism is seen as Christianity in its most dogmatic form. It appears to present itself to the world ready-armed with a panoply of creeds, doctrines and theological teachings which have developed into a formidable tradition which is both sure of itself and sure of what – and who – does and does not belong within it. The Catholic system of beliefs is often alleged to be the reason why Catholicism is found to be both irresistibly attractive to some and downright repulsive to others. Some see in their acceptance of the Catholic system a welcome end to their religious quest and the final acquisition of that certitude about the things of God which may have long eluded them; whilst for others such an acceptance would be the death of all responsible freedom of thought and expression in a field where the need and the value of personal freedom is surely paramount. For these reasons alone, not to mention even deeper ones, it would obviously be helpful, in any attempt to show how Catholicism works as a religion or a spirituality, if the Catholic system of beliefs could be located in the context of what I have written so far, and in such a way that its actual use might be explained and, in the light of that use, its true meaning might be clarified.

It is possible, I think, to locate the Catholic system of beliefs – of officially authentic theologoumena – in the context I have been constructing in the following brief way: it is, first and foremost, an essential accessory in the kind of faith-insight and faith-experience which the Catholic shares with Christ, and which lies at the heart of the religion of Catholicism. Catholic beliefs serve to give orthodox articulation and expression to that mystical vision of reality which is inherent in the faith-attitude, and to inspire the person of faith to live in accordance with that vision. Without the religiously dramatic and colourful background provided by the belief-system developed in Catholicism over the centuries, the vision of faith would be blank and unsustainable. A bare, contentless, solipsistically existential stance, it would lack stimulus for life and action. It would have no imaginative locus or focus. It would be inhumanly abstract. It would engage no feelings and inspire no effort. Hence it is that from the start, in the minds and hearts of Jesus' followers, the core vision of faith has sought and found such different imaginative expressions. Fired by the mystical insight of a recent convert, and in sharp contrast with his old religion of the Law, St Paul was first to start preaching the faith-vision of his new religion in the novel theological terms of a mystical incorporation in Jesus Christ and in the sharing of his faith. But supremely, of course, it was through the theologically loaded gospel accounts of the origins, life and death of Jesus himself as vindicated by his resurrection from the dead, that the new vision of reality began to unfold in the more easily accessible form of a human life-story.

It was from these normative New Testament foundations that the Catholic tradition began to be built and its theologoumenal belief-system began eventually to develop – in ever more formal and elaborate creeds, in the rigorous exclusion of heresies, in conciliar definitions, in official teachings. Here is not the place for detail. What needs to be recalled here is that all these different styles, from the New Testament to the latest doctrines defined in recent times, are the product of essentially the same kind of creative theological imagination at work, at different times and in different cultures and different intellectual modes, on the articulation and expression of the core vision of reality that was inherent in the faith of Jesus. Indeed this process must have begun even before the New Testament writings with the mind and imagination of Jesus himself, who after all had to articulate and express his own faith-vision, first, of course, to himself and then to his followers. It is remarkable that so little attention is paid to this radically human process of imaginative understanding and interpretation; and so little credit given for it. It is as if we somehow suppose that all the different human forms in which the vision of faith needed to be pictured so that it might stay alive and work effectively in the different generations were somehow directly dictated from somewhere above. We might be entitled to praise them rightly as inspired, but it is too easy to underestimate the astonishingly imaginative creativity with which so many human minds elaborated so many aspects of the truth they discerned in the vision of reality which their shared faith offered them – and not least, of course, the creative imagination of Jesus, who was the man who, so to speak, primed the theological pump from which later theologoumena so abundantly flowed.

Nowhere are the workings of the theologically creative imagination more in evidence than in the first documented contributions to the construction of the traditional Catholic system of beliefs in the New Testament writings. Following the initiative of Jesus, the writers were led to take the religious metaphors of Judaism and of other influential cultural sources such as Hellenism, and to adapt them in ways that would serve to express how they now saw the reality of the human situation in the light of the vision of it that dawned on them as they learned to share the faith of Jesus. What an early generation of Jesus' followers wrote down in the form of letters and gospels and history and exhortation was understandably seen by a later generation as the normative or 'canonical' foundation for the further imaginative construction of a growing system of creeds and beliefs which would express and support their Catholic faith in more detail, in culturally different ways, and to far wider audiences. Thus at the root of the Catholic tradition of beliefs, and as the initial stage of its construction, there will always lie the biblical writings. But throughout this lively process of development it was the faith of Jesus and the vision of reality which it entailed that remained sacrosanct; and it was the beliefs which articulated the vision at the heart of that faith which needed to find expression and acceptance.

※

But just what is involved in accepting the belief-system that belongs to the Catholic tradition? What does the act or activity of believing amount to for a Catholic? What are Catholics, together or individually, supposed to be doing when they say: 'We believe'? What, for a Catholic, does 'believing' actually mean or consist in? So much attention is usually given to the statements that serve as the 'objects' of Catholic belief, and to the intricacies of the Catholic belief-system itself, that relatively little is ever said to elucidate what it means to 'believe' them. It may be the case that believing has simply been swept up into what is understood by faith; but believing and the experience of having faith strike me as two quite distinct activities, however closely interrelated they might turn out to be. So they require distinct treatments before their interrelation can be sensibly described. That religious believing might be an activity which is significantly different from believing, for instance, that Manchester is barely two hundred miles from London, or that there is a Man in the Moon, has been insufficiently considered. The problem is that religious believing is often subjected to criteria which may be inapplicable to it, and then, of course, it is inevitably found wanting.

Perhaps a look at an updated translation of a normative creed which Catholics habitually recite might help:

Theologoumena 101

> We believe in a single God, an all-powerful Father, maker of heaven and earth, and of everything that is seen and unseen: and in a single Lord Jesus Christ, the one and only Son of God, sprung from the Father before all the ages, light from light, real God from real God, sprung not made, of the same reality as the Father: it was through his agency that everything came into being:
> he it was who, out of consideration for us human beings and for our salvation, came down from the heavens and took on flesh from Holy Spirit and Mary the Virgin; and he lived a human life and he was crucified for our sake in the time of Pontius Pilate; and he suffered and was buried and rose again on the third day according to the scriptures; and he ascended into the heavens and is sitting at the Father's right hand; and he is coming again with glory to judge living and dead; of his kingdom there will be no end:
> and in the Holy Spirit , the one with power to make things live, who comes forth from the Father, who is co-worshipped and co-glorified with Father and Son, and is the one who spoke through the prophets.
> In a single, holy, catholic and apostolic Church.
> We acknowledge a single baptism for forgiveness of sins.
> We expect a resurrection of the dead and life in the age to come. Amen.
> (The so-called *'Nicene-Constantinopolitan Creed'*)

There cannot be a more authentic expression of early Catholic belief than this thoroughly trinitarian and conciliar creed, inspired by the creed of the Council of Nicaea in AD 325, formulated by the Council of Constantinople in AD 381, and finally endorsed by the Council of Chalcedon in AD 451. The point of my slightly unfamiliar but sufficiently accurate translation is to sharpen the question I want to ask: when Catholics, together or individually as adherents of a spiritual religion, recite this basic formula, when they employ the operative verbs by which they assert that they 'believe' (or 'acknowledge' or 'expect') what is stated in the body of the text, what do they actually suppose they are doing?

It is not difficult to think of a range of answers to this question. Someone who had no connection with the Catholic tradition might suppose that Catholic believers were indulging their taste for reciting esoteric gibberish by way of a religious exercise whose purpose passeth understanding. A less angry, more charitable person might think the recital of basic beliefs was simply a way in which Catholics expressed their solidarity with one another. A so-called 'traditional' Catholic might think the question pointless, supposing, as he or she has always done, that reciting the creed is a matter of reminding themselves, in the context of worship, of the plain facts which are basic to their religion. Many Catholics might just bridle at the very asking of the question; and it is probably true that trying to get some kind of answer to the question might prove less difficult that explaining the point of it in the first place. But the reason for this, I think, is not that the question lacks point, but that it has been so seldom asked. And yet, given the prima facie peculiarity of the statements which form part of the complex and sophisticated belief-system of a spiritual religion like Catholicism, it would seem to me imperative to raise the question as a matter of some urgency. After all, how truly credible can a belief-system be, if it remains unclear what it means 'to believe' in it? Again, given the religious context and purpose of reciting the creed, what religious or spiritual value can there be in its recital if it is no more than a catalogue of plain facts? Again, it must be obvious that rather more than plain facts are being recited in a creed whose articles range from the purest theological account of what went on with God before time (and so before facts as we know them were around), via what seems to have actually happened to Jesus in the time of Pontius Pilate, to a world beyond his death, and on to life in an age still to come.

Given the limitless range of reference involved, the sheer theological and imaginative scope of the creed, and not least its religious and spiritual usage, it seems only right to look for an appropriate meaning for what is actually meant by 'We believe'. It does not appear that it means the mere acceptance of literal facts or truths, nor does it state a conviction about such facts or truths on the grounds of say-so, or hearsay, or on the basis of anything like evidence, whether diminished or indirect, or in the teeth of contrary evidence. All that would serve to reduce

Catholic 'believing' to just another example of what 'believing' usually means in everyday speech. For much of what Catholics claim to believe in their creed there could be nothing we could call evidence. It seems to me that it would be more intelligent to treat the 'We believe' of the creed as a strictly technical religious term proper to Catholicism itself, with a meaning significantly different from its common usage in both philosophy and common parlance. In other words, 'We believe' denotes a spiritual and religious activity specific to the Catholicism whose belief-system is being formally expressed. But what kind of activity might that be?

'We believe' means that Catholics – as a body of worshippers, although the same would be true of an individual who devoutly recites a creed beginning with 'I believe' – are, quite specifically, expressing their conscious and heartfelt acceptance of those imaginative elements that depict, structure and support the spiritual vision of reality of the world which belongs to the faith they share with Jesus. Their expressed beliefs – and this would be true of the many doctrinal beliefs that were developed later in the Catholic tradition – describe the way they choose to 'read' reality imaginatively in the light of their faith. The beliefs are not the same as their faith. They are the imaginative props and structure of the vision proper to Catholic faith. They depend for their meaning on their use as the supports of the Catholic faith-vision. Not, I must concede in passing, that Catholics are the only people whose lives may be inspired by a faith-vision, and perhaps by one not unlike that of Jesus of Nazareth. The world has never lacked for people of 'good faith'; and no doubt it is in their good faith that their salvation as human beings lies. Their good faith may well enjoy the support of other religious, or even non-religious, belief-systems. It is unlikely not to be backed by any kind of conscious or organized convictions. But I must confine myself to Catholics, and to their way of believing: though it is worth reflecting that we naturally assume the need for some form of saving grace if anyone is to become fully human, although this is not to say, of course, that saving grace has to consist in the Catholic virtues of faith, hope and love, or indeed in what is offered by any religion. But what we call 'good faith' – integrity, honesty, sincerity – is a basic requirement. To my mind, this fact simply confirms the profoundly human nature of the faith which I consider necessary to the understanding of Catholicism, as well as the difference I have maintained between faith and Catholic beliefs. I continue to think, however, that it is an advantage that Catholicism has such a strongly developed traditional belief-system which can provide so thoroughly imaginative a visionary hold on reality as read in the light of the faith it shares with Jesus.

This may seem an odd claim to make when we take into consideration not only the early creeds but also the elaborate proliferations of the rest of the centuries-old Catholic doctrinal tradition. What about the disparate, ill-sorted and, above all, dated elements that have found their way, at one time or another, into the system? What of the teachings about faith and reason and revelation? about the inspiration and inerrancy of the Scriptures? about the unity and trinity of God? about creation? about the immortality of the soul? about the freedom of the will? about original sin? about the dual nature of Christ? about the intricacies involved in grace and justification? about the nature and necessity of the Church? about papal infallibility? about the seven sacraments and especially about the sacrifice of the Mass? Then there are 'the Last Things' – judgement, purgatory, heaven and hell. And what about the Marian doctrines? – Mary's immaculate conception, her perpetual virginity, her assumption into heaven, even, perhaps, her share in the work of salvation. I simply list the chief elements which by now belong to the doctrinal tradition of Catholicism. What, it may be fairly asked, do all these exotic growths add to the broad, imaginative picture sketched in the creed? Or more pointedly: just what extra religious or spiritual use or meaning does this list of official doctrines have? Do they represent value added to the creed?

Similar questions about the complexity of the belief-system have been asked, not least in recent times, when the future credibility of Catholicism has been thought to depend on the simplification, or even on the 'dumbing-down', of its demanding doctrinal system, a weeding out of some of the features considered less congenial or attractive to 'the modern mind'. Some theologians have tried to establish a system of priorities – a 'hierarchy of truths', as it has been called – among doctrines, endowing some of them, not altogether unreasonably, with more importance than others. I have to say that I find such well-meant tinkerings with the Catholic doctrinal system both unconvincing and unnecessary. For one thing, I think they manage to avoid – if they are aware of it – the main issue, which is the use and meaning of 'believing' as an activity. It is this that should take priority if it is their intention to restore credibility to the doctrinal tradition. Excising or explaining away the supposedly difficult or embarrassing bits of it in deference to 'the modern mind' – hardly a primary criterion in the interpretation of traditional matters – simply misses this point. For one thing, it is not 'the modern mind' which the belief system is meant to address. Methodologically, what is needed is a procedure which will help Catholics come to terms with the teachings of their tradition as it stands – warts and all. It shows a serious lack of historical sense, not to mention of theological craft, to refuse to accept the fact that the tradition has had to make it ways through long periods of variable history and through different cultural backgrounds, and has had to respond continuously to new questions and unfamiliar challenges. Not surprisingly, the upshot is that the doctrinal tradition has incorporated or accrued elements which may seem to have little relevance now, but which were once answers to what were thought burning questions. As such, even where they might now have little appeal for Catholic believers, they retain their place, albeit perhaps a dispensable place, in the imaginative supporting picture of the Catholic faith-vision which it was always – and still is – theology's job to construct.

Of course, the Catholic belief-system may also be found to contain certain undesirable elements – undesirable, because they are simply unfitted to express the Catholic faith-vision. For instance, it seems to me a timely confirmation of my view of the real purpose and meaning of the Catholic belief-system that the Roman authorities have recently seen fit to drop the notion of Limbo. I cannot recall a similar move on their part in the past. But Limbo was a purely speculative and highly insensitive theologoumenon which succeeded in posing as a doctrine for centuries, and which caused particular distress to the families of innocent babies who died in 'original sin' before baptism could be administered, and who, along with those good people who died before Christ's salvation was available, were thereby thought to be condemned to missing out on the happiness of heaven. In fact, all that the notion of Limbo ever did was to fill a tricky gap in the fantasies which over-curious theologians devised at one time for an after-life world about which there was nothing, in any strict sense, to know. But dropping Limbo is no weak concession to the modern mind. It has been realized that it has no further part to play in the imaginative vision of reality which belongs to true faith in a God whose mystery lies precisely in the salvation of humanity; and it is good that the authorities have at last been shamed into dropping it before it got theology an even worse name than, in some circles, it already has. It is not, of course, impossible that there are other undesirable elements in the Catholic belief-system whose days are numbered.

But underlying the selective approach I have mentioned above, there is, I think, a more serious methodological error. The doctrinal tradition through which the Catholic belief system has been steadily developed is possessed of a unity not only of authenticity but also of purpose and use. As I am suggesting, it is meant to give, in all its variety, the imaginative dimensions and content which belong to the faith-vision of reality which was inspired by Jesus. This purpose and use applies to every part of the authentic tradition. Hence it must be right to interpret all those parts in the light of the overall purpose. Hence it is not methodologically correct to single out respectable elements of the tradition, and to promote some, to relegate others, or try to sweep them under the carpet of modernity, unless they prove positively undesirable. In other words, the meaning, purpose and use of the parts are to be properly understood only in the light of the meaning, purpose and use of the whole tradition – and not the other way round, where the meaning, purpose and use of the parts is assessed on what might be subjective or arbitrary criteria. It is a matter of being properly sensitive to the products of tradition, and duly conservative of them. Trees, in all their variety, are just part of the woods, but it is the woods that are important. If history happens to have left us with some unwelcome or intrusive trees, it is not for us to cut them down unless they are poisoning the system. We might easily damage the ecological balance of the whole wood – though we might well try to ensure that unsuitable trees are not planted in future.

※

So what the beliefs of Catholicism represent are products of the theological and religious imagination whose meaning, purpose and use is to give a pictorial interpretation to the vision of the real world of humankind as that world is envisaged in the saving faith of Jesus. They relay an intelligently imaginative interpretation of humankind and its world, and offer a reading of reality in which humankind can truly hope to live, a version which ultimately derives, via his native Judaism, from the imagination, mind and heart of Jesus. The belief-system represents a universally accessible ('Catholic') and authentic way in which to share actively and imaginatively in the salvific faith of Jesus. It results from a prolonged hermeneutical exercise undertaken in widely differing conditions throughout the centuries. It represents an interpretation of the real world of humankind which derives from, and which in its turn reinforces, the insight into reality involved in the visionary faith of Jesus which his followers are called to share. As such, the Catholic belief-system is not altogether unlike other imaginative 'readings' and interpretations of reality of the kind found in the sciences and elsewhere, where human imaginative intelligence has been consistently employed in building a tradition of truthful interpretations in the attempt to picture, understand and cope with the reality which surrounds humankind. Scientific readings rightly ground themselves in empirically testable data. The Catholic belief-system tests itself against the experience of what it is to be human. It differs from the scientific in that its meaning, purpose and use do not lie in discovering the origins and nature of the human world – on such topics a religious belief-system has no reason whatever to contest properly scientific findings – but in enabling believers to 'read' their world in such a way as to make it possible for them to live the difficult lives that human beings have to live with the graces of faith, hope and love which characterized Jesus of Nazareth.

In this way the belief-system results from a sustained interpretative effort on the part of serious and intelligent thinkers over the centuries to make sense of, and to give sense to, the real world of humankind. Where the sciences have their own scientific points of view, so Catholicism looks on reality from the point of view of humanity as such. It can cause no surprise if their readings of reality seem to clash – indeed they should be expected to seem to do so. The clash becomes regrettable only when it rests on an inability to see that different points of view and purposes underlie it, or on an unintelligent refusal to try to share the other point of view, or to acknowledge the possibility of other readings of reality with other purposes or other uses or other meanings.

Perhaps the deepest failure of imaginative intelligence lies in the inability, or refusal, to see the comprehensive role which interpretation plays in all human attempts to grasp different aspects of the truth about the nature of reality. It is as if reality were taken to be a totally objective and already transparent 'given', the knowledge and understanding of which consists simply in passively recording the stream of veridical impressions which it somehow gives off. It is impossible to think of any level of cognitive activity on the part of any sentient or intelligent being which conforms to such a pattern. I can only appeal to the importance of keeping a dog, or, even better, a cat. No animal-lover – perhaps no biologist – would, I think, suppose that members of what we regard as the sub-human world exercise their sentient and cognitive faculties is such a simplistic way. All living beings, it seems to me, 'read' their worlds in an active or at least reactive way. It is what is meant by their being alive, and certainly by their being 'domesticated'. And the degree of sophistication or imagination with which a being actively and reactively contributes to the reading of the reality which surrounds it determines the place on the scale of being which we – anthropocentrically, of course – tend to assign to it. Human beings are assigned the highest rank because in them the imaginative interpretation, or reading, of reality which underlies their different understandings of it (in religion, mathematics and the sciences, art, philosophy, literature, music and so on), has led to the creation of a variety of worlds, constructed as attempts to bring reality into an order in which it can be variously grasped and understood. It would be quite wrong to exempt Catholicism from this most human of processes, and its belief-system represents its effort to come to terms with reality as it sees it from its own specifically religious point of view.

But to stress the importance of interpretation without at the same time mentioning the underlying function of tradition would be a grave mistake. Total originality, I think, is not to be found in human knowledge. We are dependent on what we are bright enough to inherit from our predecessors. Every step forward in both understanding, and in coping with, the world depends on the fresh assimilation of what is somehow already the case, or already in use: on the new interpretation of the already available: on the imaginative recycling of what has been achieved before. One person's interpretation of his or her world is recognized as a genuine contribution to the understanding which someone in a later generation is seeking; and so it gets built into a tradition of interpretation – becomes a working part of a traditional understanding which then moves on to construct an even fuller understanding of the world in question. What drives the process forward is the tradition itself in the hands of those who positively accept it and use it. Tradition works as a tool and resource in the work of the imaginative interpretation and understanding of reality. Without tradition interpretation cannot begin; and without being open to further interpretation tradition soon becomes a dead weight. A religion such as Catholicism owes its worldly existence to these interdependent factors. From the start it has depended on the fresh interpretation, in the mind and imagination of Jesus, of a pre-existent tradition; and then on the painstaking construction of a whole tradition of interpretations which together express, through the changing centuries, the faith-vision of the world of humankind which it owes to him.

༄

It is impossible to proceed without raising questions about the nature and status of the traditional interpretations which have formed the Catholic system of beliefs. Just what kind of truths are they? How are they to be understood? How are we supposed to think that their truth is meant to be taken? Is it meant to be taken literally? Are they meant to be true in the way that propositions about states of affairs are taken to be true – as factually true? We have arrived at a need-to-know situation, and these are both awkward and delicate questions which have been too long ignored. I suspect that what has happened is that serious questions of truth and meaning have been quietly ignored, whilst the faith of Catholics has been fed on simple certainties. Pre-digested certainties, for those who cannot help being more or less gullible with regard to doctrinal matters, are painlessly swallowed and effortlessly assimilated. But faced with meatier questions about the truth and meaning of their doctrinal beliefs, it is easy to understand that such questions may prove too much to stomach. But certainty is not at all the same as truth or meaning. It is perfectly possible to be completely certain about something which is entirely untrue or meaningless. Certainty, I take it, is primarily a quality relating to the degree of conviction claimed by the knowing subject; and only secondarily is it a quality which is transferred to propositions and statements. To endow propositions and statements with certainty prior to the knowing subject's discovering whether they are true or meaningful, and in such a way as to pre-empt any opportunity the subject may have of deciding whether he is convinced or not, simply will not do. The cart of certainty is being put before the horse of knowledge, so to speak. In such circumstances, certainty can become a crippling obstacle to further growth in understanding. I say this, not to undermine the certainties that Catholics have been led to suppose they have about their beliefs, but to remind myself that my first priority is not to bolster Catholic certainties about the belief-system, but to ask important and wholly proper questions about the truth and meaning of the beliefs, the theologoumena, that have gone into its construction – in what way are they meant to be true?

Given that the statements that constitute the Catholic belief-system purport to describe actions or states of affairs that belong to a world which transcends the world in which we live, a religious world created by the theological imagination, a world of theologoumena, it is not possible to suppose that those statements can be taken literally. Their kind of truth, and the way in which it is meant, cannot be the same as the truth of statements we can make about the world in which we live as a result of our ordinary experimental knowledge of it. Of the transcendent religious world created by the theological imagination we have, by definition, no direct experimental knowledge, no sense experience of that world itself, nothing to make factual statements about. Nor could we have: it is an essentially imaginative world constructed by theology to express the vision of reality as it is understood in the light of the faith of Jesus which Catholics share.

These are awkward matters to deal with, if only because they do not usually arise. But they have been evaded for too long, and failure to address them can grossly mislead those who are expected to subscribe to the beliefs in question. There is also the further matter of the false opposition between religious beliefs and the findings of science. If the truth of Catholic beliefs is metaphorical, originating from the creative imagination of theologians, those beliefs and the findings of science are no longer in competition with one another. Nor are they even alternative to one another. They simply represent two quite different accounts given of reality: the one creatively imaginative, for specifically religious use, and the other experimental and open to repeated experiments, for expressly scientific purposes. The one does not threaten the other; and either or both can be held according to the kind of commitment people choose to have to the world in which they live. Nor does my suggested view seek to undermine either kind of account, and certainly not the one expressed by Catholic beliefs. Reaction against Catholic beliefs is usually based on the fact that they have been presented consistently as a direct, literal description of some other, different, metaphysical world or reality; and believers have become habituated to depending on, and finding consolation in, the certainty which its literal truth seems to guarantee them. Once the truth of their beliefs is said to be metaphorical, believers understandably feel, not only that they have been cruelly misled, but that they might just as well abandon their Catholic beliefs as no longer useful or relevant to them. This reaction would be hopelessly premature, and do no justice to the view of the Catholic belief-system I have been suggesting. Whether Catholics like it or not, it is not only historically the case that the supporting beliefs and doctrines of Catholicism were produced by the imaginative efforts of theologians (sometimes at Church Councils), but it is also impossible to suggest a human source for beliefs other than those imaginative theologians and their skill with religious metaphors.

It is crucial not to think of metaphors and the imagination as somehow belonging to a second-class form of discourse, inferior to literally meant statements and to the truths and certainties attainable by the workings of human reason and the senses. To think thus betrays a faulty appreciation of how human beings most frequently, and most vividly, manage to express themselves and run their complex lives. What is called for is a close look at metaphor. I opted earlier on for a loose and general sense of the word. By 'metaphor' I mean no more than what the word says: namely, that by the imaginative use of a linguistic or verbal artifice we creatively enhance the meaning and the truth of the reality which ordinarily confronts us by 'transferring' and applying to it expressions from some other field with whose meaning we already familiar. We 'metaphorize' – make metaphors of –

those expressions, with the result that our appreciation and our grasp of what confronts us is veridically extended and deepened by imaginative constructions. We come to see one thing better, more truly, in terms of something else. George Eliot obviously thought that this process was far more common than we realize:

> O Aristotle! If you had had the advantage of being 'the freshest modern' instead of the greatest ancient, would you not have mingled your praise of metaphorical speech as a sign of high intelligence, with a lamentation that intelligence rarely shows itself in speech without metaphor, – that we can seldom declare what a thing is, except by saying that it is something else?
> *The Mill on the Floss*, Book 2, ch. 1 (epigraph)

Aristotle's 'praise of metaphorical speech' (*Poetics*, ch. XXII, 1459a5–8) occurs in his discussion of stylistic devices in Greek tragedy. He notes how important a matter it is that the use of such devices should be appropriate. I translate:

> ... but much the greatest thing is the metaphorical; for this alone cannot be got from someone else, and is a sign of native genius; because using metaphor well is a matter of observing resemblance.

Metaphor is a verbal device, a figure of speech or writing, by which we aim at 'getting across', either to others or to ourselves, some new kind of understanding. This we do by spotting (and this is where the intelligent imagination comes into play) that an already familiar word or expression has the kind of resemblance or similarity to what we want to say or mean which will enable it to serve as a carrier or bearer for the new understanding we wish to express and promote. We take the familiar word or expression away from its normal or common use and use it in a transferred, 'metaphorized', non-literal sense. 'We can so seldom declare what a thing is, except by saying it is something else', said George Eliot, but she may be exaggerating, if only slightly. We do not appear to be using metaphor, for instance, when we are pointing out the ordinary contents of our world: hammer, nails, cat, Melissa, and so on. Our verbal intercourse with one another can get along at this wooden, literal level for some time. But then we find it helpful to shift verbal gear, so to speak, when we need to promote, not just basic acts of recognition, but the insights and understandings which we have in mind, and which we want to 'get across' to someone else. To create this effect, we take words and employ them creatively. We make metaphors of them.

This is a thoroughly creative activity, and one that appears to come entirely naturally to us, though some people are better at it than others. But then our native facility with metaphors can be practiced and improved. The speaker (I could just as well say 'writer') capitalizes on the familiarity of a word or expression – perhaps what Aristotle meant by 'observing resemblance' or similarity. With what is already familiar he creates a new setting, a new field of significance. The speaker's words could now, it would seem, be referring to a whole new world, though that world remains no more than the creation of the imaginative mind of the speaker, who is trying to get his hearer to take a fresh look at the ordinary world he is living in, or to turn his attention to its wider implications; and to do it in the light of the new world of meaning which the speaker is metaphorically creating. Through his artfully transferred use of familiar words, the speaker is suggesting – in fact, 'revealing' is probably the *mot juste* in this regard – what might be taken for another world altogether. But the speaker is not asserting the literal existence of some alternative reality. For reasons he has in mind, he is trying to enlarge and enhance – to transform, transfigure – the hearer's existing perception of his own ordinary world, or perhaps the quality of the attention he gives to the world he lives in, or perhaps the moral responsiveness a person exercises towards the world. The hearer can now see his ordinary world in the light of the speaker's newly revealed one, in the light of a new world of meaning. The speaker has revealed that the hearer's ordinary world has a new, hitherto unfamiliar, unsuspected meaning, a new 'depth' to it. He has tried to say what one world 'really and truly' is by creatively – imaginatively, poetically – endowing it with the qualities of another world, by locating it within the context of a new imaginative vision. There is only one, ordinary world, but it takes the invention of another metaphorical, religious world (say the world which is the construct of the Catholic belief-system) to focus and locate its truth and its importance in the vision of reality that belongs to the faith we share with Jesus.

We are most conscious of the metaphorical process when we meet it in the high arts of poetry and rhetoric, when a speaker or writer (or politician) is out to persuade and convince others to adopt a certain point of view, a certain way of seeing things, a new approach to their world, a new way of 'coming to terms' – imported, metaphorical terms – with the world in which they live. 'Look at it all this way ...' Rhetoric and poetry work, more or less subtly, by suggestion, by persuasion, by putting an imaginative construction on things, in order to produce whatever effect they desire. They suggest, in all kinds of ways, freshly imported verbal terms in which they want their audience and readers to revise or enlarge their perception of the world. They aim at recommending the adoption of those terms. The ways employed might include arguments of a more or less logical rigour, illustrations, stories, individual analogies; and in poetry the subtler collocation of the sound and sense of the words themselves to help to evoke the desired perception. What is happening in the use of metaphorical language is that the speaker or writer is introducing people, not directly to new factual information, or to new literal 'facts', or to some different and distinct world as such. Rather, he is revealing a fresh way of understanding the ordinary world in which the hearer or reader happens to be living. The Greeks not only had a word for the whole process, they made a minor goddess of it – *Peithô*, persuasiveness.

Such is the process which I describe as 'metaphor'. Metaphor belongs to, and indeed may be said to characterize, our human language capability. We would be lost without it. Without it, for instance, we could not say 'the sun rises' – which, literally speaking, it does not do, of course. But what happens is that the mundane act of our own getting up in the morning is imaginatively observed as having a resemblance to the appearance of the sun over the horizon; and merely by that transference of terms from ourselves to the sun, we are invited to see the world we inhabit in a new, positive and rather flattering way as the centre of our solar system. We willingly accept the invitation, non-factual, non-literal, pre-Copernican as it is. We endow ourselves with an enhanced and enlarged status – as if we were the sole focus of the sun's daytime attentions. But, literally speaking, the sun stays where it is, and we stick to revolving on our old orbit around it. This may be a trivial example, but in its minor way it shows the power of a simple metaphor to suggest and reveal a fresh and enlivening perception of ourselves and the world we live in.

But whilst we may all have easy and habitual recourse to metaphor in much of our discourse, there are those who are especially gifted in its use. According to the field in which they employ their gift, they are writers, philosophers, prophets, poets, politicians – and, because they are faced with the more difficult task of expressing what they make of the mystery of God, religious geniuses and the founders of religions. Whatever they may claim about the source of their gift for metaphor, or even about the provenance of the metaphors themselves, the effectiveness of their use of metaphor will, in human terms, directly depend on the degree or force of imagination with which those geniuses and founders can express themselves, and so communicate whatever their particular 'take' on reality happens to be. Their gift for metaphor is, in the last analysis, a personal gift. This rule applies to the human imagination of Jesus just as much as to any other 'inspired' founder. As Aristotle says, 'This alone cannot be got from someone else, and is a sign of native genius (*euphuia*)'.

Driven, inspired, by his personal insights, Jesus proved himself supremely capable of making metaphors out of his experience of our common world, and of making people understand our common world in ways that enlarge and transfigure its meaning. Of course, the sheer vividness and force of their imaginations will sometimes, perhaps often, make religious geniuses sound as if they had personal access to another, distinct realm of reality and truth. The power of their metaphors can be such that they seem to be describing another world entirely: to be giving a factual, literal account of a reality beyond the ordinary reality we have to live in. But the fact is that they live in the same old world as we all do; and it is their imaginative vision of the meaning, the significance, of our ordinary, common worlds that they are seeking to express. No doubt gifted visionaries of every kind have, in their zeal for over-investing in their own metaphors, managed to delude themselves into supposing that they are actually in direct contact with a reality other than this one. We have to be very careful not to follow them in their impossible delusion. But this critical caution does not entail, even despite the obviously crazy claims of some of them, rejecting out of hand what others might be trying to say about the meaning of the ordinary world we live in.

When it comes to the particular power or faculty of the human mind which creates the constructions and fictions of metaphor in order to enable us to express such understanding as we can have of what we find a mystery, I can see no alternative to turning to the imagination – the basic human ability to create and employ images or metaphors when faced with what is unknowable directly or what is only sensed. We have a wonderfully innate gift for creating images and functioning through images – to use our imaginations where we cannot simply use our reasoning minds to gain insight into what we do not and cannot know. The handiest account of what I mean by imagination I find in the following description given by that wild and wonderful English genius, Samuel Taylor Coleridge – the kind of imagination he calls 'secondary' (*Biographia Literaria*, ch. X). He went on to describe it, and to distinguish it sharply from the uncreative 'fancy' (*ibid*. ch. XIII):

> The imagination ... I consider either as primary, or secondary. The primary imagination I hold to be the living power and prime agent of all human perception, and as a repetition in the finite mind of the eternal act of creation in the infinite I AM. The secondary I consider as an echo of the former, coexisting with the conscious will, yet still as identical with the primary in the kind of its agency, and differing only in degree, and in the mode of its operation. It dissolves, diffuses,

dissipates, in order to re-create; or where this process is rendered impossible, yet still at all events it struggles to idealize and to unify. It is essentially vital ...
Fancy, on the contrary, has no other counters to play with, but fixities and definites. The fancy is indeed no other than a mode of memory emancipated from the order of time and space ...

I take this to mean that the primary imagination is what Coleridge calls the human mind's power to receive sense-impressions from the world about us, and out of them to create perceived images, or perceptions, from which the rational mind can then proceed to its typical work of understanding – another case of *nihil in intellectu, nisi prius in sensu*, once again. But it is Coleridge's secondary imagination, it seems to me, that exercises the imaginative creativity which produces the metaphors which constitute our religious beliefs. Significantly, its purpose is to 're-create', 'idealize', 'unify' our world in terms of something else. It is to the secondary, creative imagination that human beings must turn to provide themselves with the appropriate kind of intelligible insight when they confront the saving mystery of God: when the human mind has reached the end of its strictly reasoning tether, and still needs to come to terms – imaginative terms – with the mystery which alone can offer it the promise of fulfilment. For the kind of imagination required Coleridge coined his own strange adjective: 'esemplastic' – meaning 'moulding into a unity', or constructing a world or a limited whole. This seems to me to be pretty much what the theological imagination has done in the formation of the belief-system which express the vision of reality evoked by faith.

Yet in all this it must be remembered that necessary as the promotion of the imagination to a leading role in understanding Catholic beliefs certainly is, it is by no means sufficient. In the case of Catholicism recourse must be had to an entirely specific – in fact uniquely individual – set of imaginative insights into the mystery of God which provide Catholicism with its very foundation. These insights came to their first expression in the creative imagination of Jesus as expressions of his vision of reality in the light of his personal faith in God as the mystery which he discerned in his own humanity. Jesus, as a fully human being, also needed to come to terms with the mystery that enveloped and confronted his, and everyone's, humanity – a mystery of which his personal experience of human living and facing death made him supremely conscious. The exemplary human faith of Jesus also needed to be supported and expressed in and by his beliefs – beliefs which were based on material available in the tradition of his native Judaism, but 'metaphorized' in his imagination to give the kind of novel meaning which his co-religionists found offensive, but which his disciples were prepared to adopt. Jesus' faith involved a new vision of the saving mystery of God beyond that afforded by his native Judaism – or, as Jesus' first interpreter Paul preferred to put it, opposed to that on offer through the observance, or works, of the Law.

I have stressed the importance of metaphor and the human imagination, and their employment by Jesus, because I think a proper understanding of the Catholic belief-system requires, in the first place, that the need and the possibility of some literal 'Beyond' should be dropped. A 'Beyond', 'the next world', 'the afterlife' are not meant to be understood – simply because they cannot be understood – in any literal sense. They represent ways of expressing, through metaphor, the real purpose and value of our present world. Taken literally, they are a distraction from the life we are called on to live here and now. Taken metaphorically, they serve to bring out the fuller meaning of the present, mysterious, God-defined world in which we live. They are not meant to provide us with arcane knowledge of somewhere else, the theatre in which Catholicism really operates – where 'the action' really is. There exists humanity in the here-and-now, and there exists that mystery involved in being human which we have to call God. Catholicism finds the meaning of both of these through the humanity Jesus shares with us; and it is the purpose of the religion and the spirituality of Catholicism to bring the two into spiritually productive contact 'for us and for our salvation'. We do not need a literal 'Beyond', and we should not fall for the temptation to run to it for intellectual and moral cover – a move well described by an early teacher of mine as 'Dialling 999' – or to seek explanations of the puzzles with which life confronts us in ready-made, uncritically accepted theological concepts. In the second place, I want to understand Catholic beliefs in terms of the humanity of Jesus and all that is entailed in it (his salvific faith, religious vision, insight, mind, imagination), because in so doing I would be depending on what is most familiar, most routine, for all of us – the humanity which the whole of mankind shares with him. Then Catholicism might even be seen as a true humanism.

⁂

The construction of the Catholic system of beliefs I would liken to the act by which poetry is written, an act of the mind and the imagination and the sensibility, of intelligent sensitivity to the human condition. The writing of the poetical corpus which is the Catholic doctrinal system is the work of theology. I think it was C. S. Lewis who said that if theology was poetry, it was very bad poetry. I am unclear what criterion he may have been using, but it seems to me that it is possible to view Catholic beliefs, given their source, their nature and their invention in the minds and imaginations of so many gifted theologians, as a supremely poetical expression of human existence in all its defining dimensions. Beliefs are not just bald statements of matters of fact. They incorporate the most expressive interpretations imaginable of humankind's situation and the possibilities which are open to it. They offer a vivid enhancement of life in well-wrought theological language which is meant to lift and inspire human beings to a fuller and more fulfilling existence. Catholic beliefs make and transmit essential meaning and truth about humankind; and they do this through the use of the mind and the imagination and their own kind of heightened language. I find it difficult not to see this work as the work of religious poetry.

Indeed I would go so far as to say that if we trace the roots of the Catholic belief-system back to its roots in the mind and imagination of Jesus, it has been thoroughly poetical from the start. It would not be a wild or even unlikely way of seeing Jesus himself as a supremely religious and theological poet whose inspiration lies behind the development of the later system of those beliefs which further interpreted his strictly poetical insights into the religious character of his world. Catholic theologians went on to construct the beliefs we now hold as further poetical, pictorial renderings of the real world of humankind as revealed in the mystical insight of Jesus' visionary faith. The world of Catholic beliefs is the same world which Jesus' visionary faith bespeaks, but theologically, technically, poetically enlarged to suit the circumstances, challenges and needs of later ages.

The Catholic belief-system has grown piecemeal, but the visionary faith which lies behind its poetical construction is what has ensured that it has retained such coherence as it has developed over the centuries – the coherence we look on as 'orthodoxy'. The system can strike the believer as somewhat uneven and arbitrary. It is hard for some to see the religious connections between certain doctrines, and some doctrines will seem more outlandish than others. But there exists an inner connecting logic in Catholic beliefs which is not the logic of a philosophical system, but more the logic of a still developing poem – the logic which Vatican I referred to as 'the connection of the mysteries themselves with one another and with the final destiny of mankind' (Denzinger-Schönmetzer, #3016). This is not to say that all elements in the belief-system are equally weighty – some doctrines owe their place to some passing controversy now buried centuries deep in Catholic memory. Other elements in the system may strike a more fanciful note, or they may serve as more devotional or decorative flourishes or even as political statements – for instance, certain Marian doctrines, or strictly papal infallibility. In the growth of a great poetical tradition of beliefs these variations are perhaps only to be expected, and their sometimes surprising or alarming inclusion in the Catholic belief-system is no argument for their expulsion. Their expression may need to be balanced by further developments, and they need to be interpreted rigorously in the light of more central doctrines. So not all Catholic beliefs are equally important in the expression of the meaning of and truth involved in Jesus' faith. But undoubtedly, the central elements in the system – the doctrines of the Incarnation and the Trinity – will always offer the core imaginative pictures which serve as essential interpretations of what is entailed and meant by Jesus' visionary faith.

⁕

So Catholic beliefs, I am suggesting, are by no means mere statements or assertions of fact, but work rather as artfully and imaginatively created religious pictures or icons which, like great poetry, reveal our world to itself in terms of a vision of reality which owes its origins to the faith of Jesus which Catholics are called on to share. Their truth is that of a world with a religiously enhanced meaning. But there is one last characteristic that they have which makes them more than an optional poetical elaboration of our real world – they are also direct challenges to the way we live, because their truth and their meaning is not that of factual or scientific statements whose truth and meaning are empirically available to all. Catholic doctrines work if, and only if, the lived lives of believers who commit themselves to them conform to the demands of the picture of reality which those doctrines represent. Beliefs have a moral sting in their tail. Beliefs, if they are to be of any religious use, demand that we seriously commit ourselves to living in accordance with the visionary world which they reveal. Otherwise they can mean nothing of personal importance, and the truth they contain will remain void.

In support of this view I would summon a witness about whose intellectual integrity and seriousness only the benighted would harbour doubts. The family of Ludwig Wittgenstein had Jewish roots which Ludwig's grandfather, Hermann Christian, had deliberately cut by the mid-nineteenth century, the better to integrate into Viennese society. It was Ludwig's father, Karl, who became one of the richest men in the Austro-Hungarian Empire, a leading figure in the world's iron and steel industry. Ludwig's mother, Leopoldine Kalmus, herself partly Jewish, was a Catholic who furthered the assimilation of the family into Viennese cultural life. Intensely musical, she saw to it that evenings at the Palais Wittgenstein were enlivened by the likes of Brahms, Mahler and Bruno Walter. So Ludwig, the eighth and youngest child of this remarkable family, had a religious pedigree which included Judaism and Catholicism. Thought to have a bent for engineering, at the age of fourteen he was sent to the technical *Realschule* in Linz, where – fascinatingly – Adolf Hitler was a contemporary. But Wittgenstein's later commitments to engineering, mathematics and philosophy never erased a personal concern about Catholicism.

In his *Culture and Value* (in fact the translation of a selection of his *Vermischte Bemerkungen* [Miscellaneous Remarks], Blackwell 1980), he often refers to Christianity in ways that show a serious and sympathetic understanding of it. But it is clear that the systematic beliefs and doctrines of Catholicism simply could not work for him – that is, as he explains, his way of life did not conform to the demands of the vision of Catholic faith. I translate an extract written in 1937:

> In religion it has got to be the case that to each stage of religiousness there should correspond a sort of expression which makes no sense at a lower stage. This doctrine [Wittgenstein is thinking of predestination] which is meaningful at a higher stage, is null and void for a man who is at present standing on a lower stage – it can be understood only *wrongly*, and so these words have *no* validity for this person.
> For example, Paul's doctrine of predestination is, at my stage, irreligiousness – hateful nonsense. So it is no good for me, because I can make only a wrong use of the picture it offers me. If the picture is to be pious and good, then that is so at a completely different stage, at which it has to be made use of in life completely differently from the way I could use it.
> (p. 32, his italics)

Wittgenstein appears to be saying, among other things, that the truth and meaning of systematic beliefs and doctrines depends on, and corresponds to, the level of religious development or maturity or performance a person has attained in his life; that religious maturity has to do with no longer having to take beliefs and doctrines literally; that taken literally (as they must be by someone who can know no better), they can be irreligious nonsense. There would be a great deal to be learnt from this and other remarks of Wittgenstein on religious belief. He treats religious believing seriously as an activity that deserves attention in its own right, and he sees the problem of both the distinction and the connection between holding beliefs and living a life of faith. I translate just one more remark of his:

> I read: 'no one can say "Jesus is Lord" except by the Holy Spirit' (1 Corinthians 12:3). And it is true: I cannot call him *Lord*, because that says absolutely nothing to me. I could call him 'the Exemplar', even 'God'– or actually I can understand, when he is given such names. But the word 'Lord' I cannot pronounce with meaning. *Because I do not believe* that he will come to judge me – because *that* says nothing to me. And it could say something to me, if I lived *entirely* differently.
> (p. 33, his italics)

Whether articles of belief like 'Jesus is Lord' (often said to be the earliest form of the Creed), or doctrines like the Judgement can be religiously true, can be meaningfully affirmed as true, and can have any effective use, ultimately depends, in other words, on the spiritual quality of the life one is prepared to live. It is only a life lived with the faith-vision of Jesus that validates the beliefs of the Catholic tradition which have been framed to support and express it. Faith and beliefs are distinct but related factors in Catholicism.

Perhaps the chief objection to my suggestions about the nature and use of Catholic beliefs is bound to centre on what appears to be the loss of what I have called the Beyond – that actual, parallel but transcendent world where we shall all hope to find our fulfilment, and without which we suppose that our ordinary world lacks its proper significance. To such an objection I can only say that such a realm, far from validating the world we live in, seems to me to reduce it to a level of insignificance which undermines the unique value with which Catholic beliefs are precisely constructed to endow it and enhance it. At some point we have to wean ourselves from an infantile dependence on the Beyond, and learn to live our real, this-worldly lives in the visionary light of faith which our Catholic beliefs cast on humankind. 'Men of Galilee, why do you stand looking up towards heaven ...?' (Acts 1:11). Or, to conclude with wise words from the philosopher John Rawls:

> The perspective of eternity is not a perspective from a certain place beyond the world, nor the point of view of a transcendent being; rather it is a certain form of thought and feeling that rational beings can adopt within the world. And having done so, they can, whatever their generation, bring together into one scheme all individual perspectives and arrive together at regulative principles that can be affirmed by everyone as he lives by them, each from his own standpoint. Purity of heart, if one could attain it, would be to see clearly and to act with grace and self-command from this point of view.

This remarkable statement displays much – but not all – of the view of Catholicism which I am trying to recommend.

Chapter 4

Salvation

It might perhaps strike some as strange that there is, among the formally defined theologoumena of the Catholic doctrinal tradition, no single dogmatic definition of what salvation consists in. Perhaps in the case of what is so spiritual a matter, and so personal an experience, no definition is either possible or even desirable. Perhaps we owe it to some modest reserve on the part of theologians that, at least in this instance, they stuck to the limits of their craft and left what was beyond them well alone. So never, as far as I can see, has it been deemed necessary by the authoritative guardians of the tradition, whether they were taking their first steps into a pagan world or in their later confrontations with heresy, to declare formally what the salvation which Catholicism offers actually consists in or amounts to. Among the traditional theologoumena, the chief doctrines of Catholicism, there are, of course, a multitude of firmly formulated declarations relating to the ways in which Catholics are to believe that they can achieve salvation – above all, through the unique union of the divine and the human in Christ their Saviour, and in the saving power of his sacrificial life and death and resurrection, through sharing Christ's Holy Spirit in their cooperation with divine grace, through the workings of the Church and the sacraments, with the support of Mary and the saints, and so on. On the necessary and available means of being saved there is no shortage of clearly framed dogmas; but as to what the end – salvation itself – actually amounts to, or what its factual value is 'on the ground' when we try to 'cash' the idea of salvation, there is nothing defined at all. What we do have, however, is a wonderful range of imaginative theologoumena which indicate how salvation may be pictured.

Now I can quite understand why some might think that in remarking on this absence of clear dogmatic definition regarding salvation I am forgetting everything that is said, perfectly clearly, in the Catholic doctrinal tradition about what still lies ahead of us after death – 'we look', according to the Creed, 'for the resurrection of the dead and the life of the world to come'. That, surely, is what salvation consists in – that is the end to which the defined means mentioned above are meant to be bringing us. To this response I have two comments to make: first, defined and conclusively definite as 'the resurrection of the dead and the life of the world to come' may sound, we are left, in fact, none the wiser about what they might actually amount to or consist in. We simply do not – and at present, cannot – know what may be supposed to happen at the resurrection of the dead or in the world to come. Slow motion action replays are not available for descriptive analysis and comment. Second, to postpone the achievement of salvation until after death is both to limit its real effectiveness to 'the next life', and to diminish its efficacy in our present condition. Surely Catholicism would claim to help people to improve, not least spiritually, in this life, to begin to enjoy whatever the benefits of salvation may be supposed to consist in while they are still alive. After all, the Catholic authorities and preachers are loud in their claims that being a Catholic is spiritually beneficial for the soul here and now. But in precisely what actual ways? It is a fair question and, to my mind, a necessary one – not least if I am going to be able to explain just how I think Catholicism should work as a spirituality, as a way to personal salvation. Catholicism offers its own particular form of salvation, and I wish to know just what that salvation actually is. If it reduces this present world to (at best) a dummy run, or an obstacle course, which may eventually lead to some reality still to come, so that this world becomes a place where Catholic observance counts for no more than the dress rehearsal for the still unknowable show which only starts when the curtain goes up after death, then Catholicism would find itself in trouble from many angles. Are we, in this world, only 'going through the motions' spiritually, prior to the achievement of salvation in the next? Does the salvation offered by Catholicism, which claims to correspond to the needs of the whole of humankind, make no real earthly difference to people?

⁂

So what difference might it make? The difficulty we experience in trying to say what the difference actually is has much to do with the metaphorical character of the language inevitably involved in the theology of salvation. I have argued for the metaphorical character of all theologoumena, all doctrinal and theological language usage; but perhaps its metaphorical character is nowhere more intense than in the matter of salvation. In other areas Catholic theology has acquired, usually through the demands of controversy, a certain technical polish, a quasi-philosophical refinement (for instance: the use of abstractly sophisticated terms such as nature, person, relations, properties, circumincession, hypostatic union, transubstantiation, predestination, immortality, and so forth). But these impressive advances in expression, it seems to me, might be quite as misleading as they are helpful, insofar as they pretend that some sort of literal and conclusive accuracy is attainable – and has been in fact attained – in the theological fields where they operate. That is one of the chief ways in which metaphors may be deemed successful – by the way they manage to keep their ineradicably metaphorical character well masked. But a theological term cannot shed its metaphorical character simply by sounding technical. It remains a term transferred or concocted – but still metaphorized – from some other field of expression and put to work in the theological field where all terms are, as I have maintained, systematically out of their literal depth. Now with salvation the case is somewhat different. Salvation has never been subjected to dogmatic definition, presumably because, for one thing, the basic centrality of the idea of salvation in Catholicism has never been seriously questioned. Indeed it could hardly be questioned without questioning whether

Catholicism is a seriously spiritual religion at all. So salvation retains all the vividness and strength of what we might call an undefined or primary metaphor; and this is one of the reasons why the difference it actually makes has been taken for granted and still requires some explanation.

In fact, of course, salvation, as expressed in Catholicism, stands in the midst of a cluster of associated metaphors which together seek to express what Catholic salvation is believed to amount to. Salvation has worked as a metaphor which attracts and triggers the use of other metaphors: for instance, the metaphor which speaks of salvation in terms of a God-given fulfilment of humankind's basic and defining needs and aspirations, further elaborated as the sanctification or the holiness or the integrity achieved in a final union with God's mystery, or in the achievement of the 'beatific vision' in heaven which follows our resurrection from the dead. Here the stress is on the attainment of our personal completion or perfection, on a personal resurrection from our native deadness, on our finally becoming the person each of us was meant to be all along. Other metaphors for salvation have a less positive emphasis, centring more on the eventual overcoming of our inherent shortcomings. Thus we are said to undergo redemption, that is, being freed at a price from our enslavement to sin; or to be reconciled with God after showing ourselves to be hostile towards him and being alienated from him by sin; or to be justified or vindicated after sinfulness has called our innocence into question; and, of course, the word 'salvation' itself betokens our preservation or rescue from the destructive effects of sin and the shipwreck of a Godless life. What is interesting to note is the unmistakeably dramatic quality of all these metaphors, whether they are more or less positive in their implications. They succeed in conveying a sense of crisis – of our having to face some critical test which our personal integrity might fail if it does not receive assistance which it is not in our own power to supply. Salvation is no easy matter, and the metaphors which are associated with it do not picture it as such.

Serious people universally admit that we can all tend to put obstacles in the way of our own salvation. If there is one general human characteristic which has been widely present all along – and is still as rampant as ever – it is surely an overall penchant for self-destruction. It is with this that Catholic salvation is locked in combat: with a humanity which is, when it wants to be, blind and deaf to its own basic need for salvation, to its own crippled inability to save itself, to its inherent selfishness, its intellectual obtuseness, its dire lack of imagination, its besetting moral weakness – in theological parlance, its inclination to sin, which is seen as an offence against a God whose mystery can alone rectify and salvage a humanity which has fallen away from the state of coherent integrity in which God is believed to have originally created it, and in the maintenance and development of which God remains a necessary element. Thus the metaphors for salvation work against an intensely dramatic background, a cosmic struggle between sin and God which graphically expresses the individual condition of every human being. It takes metaphors to express this crucial drama. It may be felt that my stress on the metaphors of salvation, and on the metaphorical character of doctrinal and theological language in general, is in some way calculated to undermine the actual reality of what is at issue here. On the contrary: without metaphors what else could be said to put us, and keep us, in the dramatic picture which Catholicism paints of our salvation? All the same, it still has to be asked how salvation might be thought to work, and what actual effect it has.

These questions are all the more pressing because salvation is not pictured as an instantaneous event but as involving us in a spiritual process of transformation at God's hands over time during this life (e.g., Romans 12:2; 2 Corinthians 3:18). The saving of one's soul – another dramatic touch – normally needs to come about through the gradual changes wrought by the inward conversion (*metanoia*) of one's life from ways of sin to the way of God. But this radical process will occur only if we willingly cooperate with God in bringing it about. God is pictured as being on continual stand-by, in the wings, ever ready to contribute his help in the form of those gifts of his own Spirit which are called grace. Grace is constantly needed to assist and boost the feeble and ineffectual efforts at achieving our salvation which are the best we can ever hope to produce. Grace – the transforming power of the mystery within our humanity which we call God – brings about results which are quite beyond the scope of our own powers and resources. Only God can impart the increasing 'godliness' or holiness which leads towards the salvation which alone will repair our faulty human condition and bring it to its true and proper state. Once again in its doctrinal and theological language Catholicism presents the working of personal salvation in lively metaphorical theologoumena which express a necessary but unequal interplay between our imperfect selves (or souls) and the saving power of God's mystery. Theological metaphors build an effective scenario where salvation is presented as an ongoing drama between the human soul and God. But whilst the drama lacks nothing either in grandeur or in truth, it may still be asked what it all actually amounts to in terms of change to the condition and behaviour of the individual who is saved. How does it work, and what difference does it make?

※

But before trying to find an answer to these questions, and whilst I am on the subject of Catholicism's doctrinal and theological metaphors for the drama of salvation, I would like to deal with what, in my view, is the most outstanding salvation metaphor of them all – the doctrine of the Holy Trinity. I am aware that the sudden appearance of the Trinity in this context is bound to surprise and even alarm people. The reason for their consternation is, I think, quite simple. If the doctrine of the Trinity has figured in their understanding of Catholicism at all, it is usually to be found somewhere on its margins; or, more usually, dragged in as a desperate last-minute adjustment to a fundamentally theistic concept of God. For all the ceaseless use of the sign of the Cross – an overtly Trinitarian practice – and the employment of the names of Father, Son and Spirit in the public liturgy and in private prayers and devotions, Catholics seem almost to have lost hope of coming to intelligent terms with the supreme mystery of the three-in-oneness which definitively characterizes the God of their salvation. Perhaps an occasional misleading analogy recalled from childhood – the Trinity is like my memory, my understanding and my will, which are the three powers of my one soul; or (perhaps better) like St Patrick's shamrock – further garbled by a roughly annual, ill-judged sermon on Trinity Sunday, casting even more dubious obscurity over the subject (*obscurum per obscurius*), has been all the help most church-going Catholics have been given. The Trinity has been abandoned to the professional curiosity of theologians; and most of them, it must be said, seem to have succeeded in making nothing more than an impenetrable conundrum of it, whilst giving the impression that they were in some way privy to the inner workings of what they seemed to suppose is the divine nature.

But the truth and the meaning of the Catholic doctrine of the Trinity is to be found, I believe, not somewhere in the unfathomable depths of divinity, but simply in the way Catholics believe their God works his salvation. It is all too easy to lose sight of the necessarily metaphorical character of traditional doctrinal theologoumena, and to be distracted into taking them literally and then speculating pointlessly on what they might then mean and how they might be true. All that has happened is that one serious error has been compounded with another. In any case, it is difficult to suppose that such barren procedures could give rise to any serious religious or spiritual values. It is interesting to note that while the basis for the later doctrine of the Trinity was firmly embedded in the New Testament writings – they could hardly have been written without Father, Son and Spirit being prominent in the contemporary usage – the Trinity was not considered a matter for speculation. Rather, the threefoldness of the Christian God had much more to do with determining the practical shape of the early creeds and baptismal formulas. For two or three centuries it is safe to say that, apart from trying their hand at a few clumsy analogies and some brave but unenlightening terminology (substance, person), early theologians understood the Trinity, not in terms of the mysterious internal life of God, but in terms of God's external functioning as Saviour – a function in which that of Creator served as the first, necessary stage. The Son and the Spirit were represented as active along with the Father in the work – or 'economy', as it was technically called – of both creation and salvation. Irenaeus of Lyons, quite the best of early theologians apart from Origen, writes vividly of the Son and the Spirit as the two 'hands' which God extrapolates when there is such 'external' divine work to be done. But of course this functional extrapolation entails self-revelation on God's part. From the way God works as a Trinity can be glimpsed the way God's mystery must somehow be in itself; and in time, under the pressure of controversy about the divine status of the Son and the Spirit, the curiosity of theologians was diverted from the working of salvation towards speculation about the workings of the internal Trinitarian life of God. But it remains true that from the start the characteristic Catholic doctrine of the Trinity had its origins in the way the divine work of creation and salvation was envisaged. To reconnect the doctrine of the Trinity with the work of salvation simply restores it to its proper place in the Catholic tradition.

It is clear from the theological metaphors for salvation which I mentioned earlier that God is pictured as a God who, above all else, is intimately involved in the work of salvation. The process of salvation, metaphorically expressed, is anything but superficial or mechanical or impersonal. In a variety of scenarios, the human soul in need of salvation is brought into direct personal confrontation and contact with God its Saviour in a more or less dramatic but always close encounter. God intervenes on the soul's behalf – involves himself intimately in the soul's salvation – whether that salvation is portrayed as the fulfilment of the soul's basic needs or as its sanctification or as its redemption from sin or as its justification and vindication from charges of guilt, or as its gradual transformation into godliness by the power of divine grace, or as the salvaging of the soul from its wrecked condition. In the Catholic doctrinal and theological tradition, salvation at the hands of God is seen as affecting the most intimate depths of the soul imaginable; and the doctrine of the Trinity furnishes an unsurpassable model of divine involvement in the work of human salvation at the deepest possible level.

Now I would contend that that the supreme doctrinal metaphor of the Trinity is wholly to do with this 'personal' involvement of God in our salvation. In fact, I would go so far as to say that the doctrine of the Trinity is primarily meant to present a picture of the theological shape or form of our salvation. Hence, for one thing, the effect which the doctrine has had on the shape or form of fundamental Catholic practices: on the tripartite creeds which rehearse Catholic beliefs about the creator Father, the redeemer Son and the sanctifying Spirit; on baptism in the names of Father, Son and Spirit; and on the ubiquitous sign of the Cross. Salvation, in the Catholic tradition, is not presented as being a vague or remote procedure. It is as deep a spiritual process as can be imagined. It consists, in its theological and metaphorical dress, in our coming to share willingly, through supportive God-given grace, in the indwelling and hallowing Spirit of God 'in person' – the Spirit who is the none other than the Son-of-the Father's Spirit, and who therefore draws us into the reality of the mystery we are constrained to call God insofar as it has been granted to us to imagine that mystery as three divine persons actively engaged in the work of our salvation. Such is the measure of God's involvement in our salvation, and in the Catholic tradition salvation is nowhere better, or more clearly, expressed than in the doctrine of the Trinity.

Of course it is also the case that this approach to the doctrine of the Trinity as a theological and metaphorical expression of our salvation was bound to stimulate theological speculation further. It may seem understandable that curious theologians should begin to suppose that if our salvation is the effect of the trinitarian working of God's mystery, then God, still conceived as the unreconstructed God of theism, thereby reveals the further fact about himself that he is a Trinity – that his unique Godhead actually exists as three 'persons'. But theologians were, as so often, forgetting the limitations inherent in their craft. At the very point where they should have respected the metaphor of the saving Trinity most carefully, theologians fell for their besetting temptation of engaging in the kind of metaphysical literalism and fundamentalism which theism can encourage. They considered themselves licenced to begin to describe the inner life of their God, forgetting the non-descriptive, metaphorical nature of their work. Once this move was made, it was a short step to the elaborate proliferations of a trinitarian terminology which, still familiar as it may be to some, makes no sense outside its own mistaken field – nature, persons (nothing usefully to do with what we have come to mean by an individual person; otherwise we would have three gods), subsistent relations, properties, co-inherence, circumincession or perichoresis, and so forth. None of this intrusive prying into a divine entity cast any further light on the mystery of our salvation so vividly expressed in the metaphor of the trinitarian mystery which draws us into the Son's love of the Father by the gift of the Spirit who is the perfect love mutually existing between them. Seen in this way, in its full metaphorical colours and without any metaphysical literalism, the Trinity shines out as the master metaphor of our Catholic salvation, of which the other dramatic metaphors for salvation mentioned above turn out to be but thin, pale and partial reflections.

Indeed I have been sometimes led to wonder whether in Catholicism the Trinity is not such a dominant and satisfying metaphor for salvation that it has rendered the name God as a metaphor for the ultimate salvific mystery religiously and spiritually redundant. Should Catholics speak of God at all? If we are not bold enough to replace God with the Trinity, are we not missing the most important point that Catholicism has to make? – is it not the case that its unique inspiration Jesus, revealed, in re-imagining God, a radically new approach to the salvation of humankind – to be developed only later, of course, into the doctrine of the Trinity – an approach to humanity's saving involvement in mystery which is so startlingly novel and intimate that it makes other religious approaches to some Saviour God quaintly obsolete? Has not God been replaced by the Trinity? Outrageous-sounding questions, I freely admit: but not so outrageous when you think that what Catholics believe they depend on for their salvation is not at all the metaphor of a distant deity, but the unity of a Trinity into whose eternally intimate relationships – Father, Son and Spirit – they are afforded spiritual access through their saving adherence to Jesus. I would go so far as to say that in Catholicism salvation and the Trinity are different but synonymous metaphors – rather as Isaiah identified the new vision of his God with his salvation, when he sang:

> Surely God is my salvation;
>   I will trust, and will not be afraid,
> For the LORD GOD is my strength and my might;
>   he has become my salvation.
> With joy you will draw water from the wells of salvation ...
>   for great in your midst is the Holy One of Israel.'
>   (Isaiah 12:2–3,6)

The Trinity is Catholic salvation theologically pictured in the vivid metaphors of interrelated divine persons, all three distinctly involved in a saving unity within which we are enabled to live and to respond more fully to the mystery of our being human.

※

But however much the galaxy of Catholic theological metaphors for salvation, with the Trinity at its core, is to serve a useful and meaningful purpose, it still remains the case that, whatever it is that salvation is pictured as bestowing on humankind, it must address and mesh with the actual condition in which humankind finds itself. We cannot avoid the questions: precisely what is salvation a salvation from? On what does it have an effect? And what is that effect? How are we to suppose that the process of salvation works in practice? To try to give an account of salvation as central to the religion of Catholicism, and to try to appreciate the full power and depth of the religious metaphors involved in that account, is one thing: but to account for what it actually effects is another. True as it is that we are dealing with spiritual matters, we are not thereby exempted from rendering as clear an account as we can of what is meant to be happening when we are being saved. To do this, there needs to be some account given of the human condition. But reasonable accounts of the human condition, and particularly accounts which are not already religiously loaded in favour of the need for salvation, are perhaps not all that easy to come by. The hoped-for answer required tends to frame the problem described. Yet it may be the case that, given the limits of human thinking, this is a benign and inevitable logical circularity.

Of course, a salvation religion like Catholicism does not concern itself primarily with the logical niceties of its position – salvation is salvation from sin. The human condition – and the biblical creation myth of the Fall is there to show it – is one of alienation, whether native or deliberate, from God; and so salvation primarily involves the overcoming of this alienation. If it is right to think of God as the mystery involved in being human, then the fallen human condition amounts to being alienated from what is most deeply true of oneself; and salvation involves the recovery of one's own existential mystery. But whilst I think it would be stupid to ignore what theology means by the sinfulness of the human condition, I have to remind myself, once again, that in speaking of sin as an offence against God I am dealing with a theologoumenon. Sin, thus considered, seems to me to give a perfectly sound and veridical account of the human condition – in its metaphorical way. But is it possible (as I believe it must be) to give a more non-theological account of the condition which is addressed by the salvation which Catholicism has to offer? If this cannot be done, I cannot see how I can ever hope to be in position to say how Catholicism actually works, as I maintain I ought to be able to do. How could Catholicism address the world outside itself if it has to remain locked in its own circle of metaphors? Can those metaphors work – that is, be meaningful and true – only for religious insiders? Are they not meant to touch the human condition at large – not least in a religion which calls itself 'Catholic'?

Abstract attempts to describe the human condition must be legion, but they are not what we need for our purpose.

It is, strictly speaking, not the human condition – however it may be described – that is relevant here. The idea is too general to be manageably useful. What I think is called for – and here I am quite aware that I am loading the enquiry in my own favour, but only because I can see no other worthwhile way of proceeding – is some plausible account of the *personal experience of being human* – that is, an account of what it is like for someone to feel their own humanity, their way of being human, an account that I would call *existential*. Now such an account can only be profoundly subjective. In fact, it might be said that the more profoundly subjective it was, the better – if it were not subjective, it would invalidate itself as yet another objectivizing and generalizing account of the human condition. But unless Catholicism can somehow be connected with an acceptable account of the experience of being human, it will not be possible to say how it is supposed actually to affect the business of being human – how it works as a salvation religion. It is if, and only if, Catholicism can be securely rooted in a recognizably concrete experience of being human that it deserves to survive and exercise its saving function in human life. In what ways does Catholicism have the necessary answers to questions raised by our experience of being human? If it has no such answers, then it seems to me to have no real role to play in human salvation. It deserves the fate of the fig tree in the parable which had produced no fruit for three years: 'Cut it down! Why should it be wasting the soil?' – although, to stick with parable, perhaps the gardener's suggestion that an extra year and some well-administered fertilizer might possibly produce results: 'If it bears fruit next year, well and good; but if not, you can cut it down' (Luke 13:6–9).

Clearly we have reached a crucial point in this essay. On the one hand, I have been demanding that Catholicism should have its roots embedded in humanity and have its saving effect on the experience of being human. On the other hand, it hardly seems likely that we could ever reach an agreement about what the experience of being human amounts to. But I wonder whether the difficulty over the experience of being human has more to do with the fact that many, perhaps most, people have never taken the time or opportunity to reflect on an experience which must be accessible in one form or another to any serious person – I mean on the concrete, personal experience of what it is to exist as a human being. It seems to me that I can proceed only on the basis of what I personally find this experience to be like in my own case, and what I have learned (and perhaps failed to learn) from it. This experience, apart from the overall subjectivity of it which I have freely admitted, is conditioned by genes, education, temperament, employment, and whatever other factors determine the way people construct and view their worlds and themselves and their relationships with, and dependencies on, others in their worlds. So the experience will be radically individual, without being solipsistic, as well as subjective. But I do not see that these qualities need invalidate it. After all, from where else but from serious reflection on one's own personal experience of being human might a reasonable view of what it is to be human emerge? – unless, of course, one is to settle for some second-hand, reach-me-down description derived from someone else's religion or philosophy? So critically aware as I think I am of the inherent limitations of my own – and anybody else's – 'reading' of the experience of being human, and without more ado, I shall boldly venture to offer what I think I have learned from my own experience in my own case. I am also well aware that my view may tell people more about my personal weaknesses than about any strengths I may have – but then whose honest view of humanity can avoid being self-revealing? And again: I have to hope that the terms in which I describe my experience of my own existence as a human being might – who knows? – ring at least a faint bell in others.

Very roughly speaking, I would maintain that being human, as experienced by a serious human being, may be said to involve a potential, a need, and an aspiration for personal, intellectual and spiritual (including moral) growth and well-being, in addition to a common and regular tendency to fail to fulfil these basic aims. I have to suppose that this view is to some extent pre-conditioned by my native Catholicism. It would be odd if it were not.

But it would be impossible, even undesirable, to try to eliminate all the influences to which I have been subjected. I cannot see many honest human beings, even if they might express their reading of human nature differently, completely rejecting the basic picture of humanity I have sketched. I would like to think that the salvation offered by Catholicism constitutes a direct attempt to speak to all aspects of such an experience, and to provide the support and encouragement that humankind needs to overcome failure in them and achieve their fuller development. But it is probably true that Catholicism, as commonly presented, has emphasized the overcoming of moral failure – salvation from sin – at the expense of openly fostering the more positive ideals and aims that appear to form part of being human. If so, it has no doubt done so in a thoroughly practical, not to say pastorally realistic, spirit. Salvation has to start somewhere, and if failures are not firmly dealt with, then success with humankind's more positive aims can hardly be expected. In fact, of course, the negative and positive aspects of being human are not so neatly distinguishable. To overcome failure is already the beginnings of growth.

If I pause and think of myself as subject, so to speak, to what is perhaps best called the pressure of existence, as existing under the weight of simply being, I find I am led to imagine (note the word – this is in no sense a scientific analysis, though it has an experiential base) that my experience of human existence is most clearly expressed in terms of certain *necessities* or *imperatives*. I am not suggesting that this 'analysis' of the human condition is based on anything other that what I happen to find it feels like to exist as a human being, when I take time and opportunity to think about it. I am not speaking of the particular burdens of my personal failures and shortcomings (which are many but boring); nor about an experience which is in any way psychologically depressing – in fact, I find it intriguing. I am trying to speak of what I find it is like simply to exist. If readers find this a weird procedure, I can only suggest that this may be because they have never stopped to feel and think about how they experience the deeper dimensions of their own humanity. Let them try it for themselves, and they may come to imagine the matter differently, of course, and different findings will impose themselves. I am assuming that this kind of existential introspection is a procedure open to anyone with normal human reflective consciousness, and with the opportunity to conduct it. All I am saying is that in my case I find I experience my existence in terms of certain necessities or imperatives which impose themselves on me.

These necessities ('imperatives' may suggest that I feel that someone else is ordering me about, which is not at all what I experience) are not vague or characterless. In fact they can be easily, if very crudely, classified as physical, intellectual and moral. I experience my being human, in other words, as being under three kinds of necessity – and not just some necessity or compulsion in a relatively superficial sense which might compromise what we ordinarily understand as freedom of the will or liberty of action. I am speaking of three deeper-set necessities which belong, are positively part of, the individual person I am as a sharer in humankind, in simply being human. I am quite sure that there may well be better, more cogent, less arbitrary and home-spun, more philosophically (and psychologically) sophisticated ways of putting all this – as I have said, I am simply giving imaginative expression to what, in my experience, I find it feels like to be human. I am also quite sure that I must be reading into the experience structures which are derived from various other sources. I am imaginatively constructing my view of the human condition from pre-existing materials found elsewhere. Far from being embarrassed by this, I fail to see how, without the imaginative importation of ideas from elsewhere (or metaphors, as they are more properly called), any usefully articulate interpretation of the experience of being human is possible. After all, which of us can locate ourselves right outside our own given humanity and deliver timelessly objective judgments on it from some lofty, external standpoint? It is at junctures such as this that the imagination has to be called on to boost the limited range of reason in order to project further the trajectory of our knowledge and our self-understanding.

I think that what I am in fact doing is pointing out, on

the basis of my own experience, what certain philosophers sometimes refer to as 'transcendentals'. A transcendental, as I understand it, is a quality which something possesses as an absolute condition of its own possibility – in other words, a constitutive sine qua non, a quality without which it would be impossible for it to exist as the thing that it actually is. In experience these come over as the necessities I have listed. I find that it would be impossible for me to be the human person that I actually am without them – without the physical, intellectual and moral necessities that I experience. This would be true, I think, of any who count themselves human. We would all be lost without them. But it seems to me that their presence is not simply some philosophical embellishment of existing human nature. The transcendental necessities represent precise points in human experience where humankind finds itself in permanent need, if it is to grow into its potential, of fulfilling them as demands laid upon it by its own actual existence. They are the existential springboards from which it is necessary for us to leap beyond ourselves, if we seriously want to become ourselves; and from which it is impossible to retreat, unless we no longer want to be who and what we find we can be. They are the bases of those acts of self-transcendence which we can and do so often resist, but which are demanded of us if we wish to survive and grow. They are also the points at which the Catholic virtues of faith, hope and love mesh, so to speak, into what is most definingly human about us, and support and facilitate those acts of self-transcendence which bring us towards our salvation.

※

Whilst there are several physical necessities to which humankind is subject, such as the limitations of space and time, as well as the need for food, clothing, shelter, and the like, for the seriously thoughtful human being the chief necessity must be that of facing death as the end of the physical existence we now enjoy. This can seem a truly fearsome necessity, bringing about, for all we actually know, the annihilation of our physical reality and the disintegration of 'the limited whole' which is the world we have made our own. Worse: as it stands, it seems a truly desperate necessity, prompting justifiable reactions of hopelessness and outrage. But, looked at more dispassionately, the presence and pressure of death are far from confined to the end of life. Death is a transcendental quality of human life – an absolute condition of the possibility of existing as the kind of human beings we actually are. Without death the very meaning of being human would be completely changed. However long we avoid paying attention to it, death exercises its influence on the whole process of human living; and wise are those who learn to keep the thought of death constantly in mind. It casts its spell and its shadow over everything we are and do. However remarkable our abilities, our talents and achievements, we can be sure that they will one day come to a full stop. Death, in any case, is with us all the time in the deaths of family, of friends, of those swept away in war or natural disasters, of victims of sickness, crime and accident, of the prominent and the humble, even of beloved pets.

There is more to be said about how Catholicism works to save us from the oppression of death; but it is worth noting now that Catholicism makes no denial of the inexorability of death or of its effects. The crucified and dying figure on the Cross is kept firmly and permanently before Catholic eyes. The necessity of death cannot be avoided. Death can only be overcome by its being transformed, in the boldest of paradoxes, into the means towards fuller living. What begins to work this transformation is the grace and virtue of hope. With hope the character of death is changed so radically that our actual death-bound life becomes a life-bound dying. Death is thereby robbed completely, not of its physical necessity, but of its spiritually oppressive dominance over life. Where death prevailed before, there is hope; and where there is hope, there is life. Where there is no hope, we must either succumb to the final dominance of death, or at best brace ourselves to confront death at the end in the bleak, fatalistic spirit of Stoicism – perhaps the best defence against the need to die that desperate human reason can provide. Catholicism offers a salvation from physical death which works through hope and trust.

But a timely word of warning. I think it is fair to say that the Catholic imagery regarding the fuller life to which hope leads us is notably graphic. It vividly presents that life in terms of an eternal world in which we live a further life for ever after death. The solemn judgement, the joys of heaven, the pains of hell, the boundless and beatific life of God's own eternity – nothing is lost in the telling. And very understandably so: it would be impossible to find a better way of celebrating victory over the physical necessity of death than imagining the continuance of a far richer life. But we have to realize that we have suddenly passed beyond the reach of reason into the realms of trust and hope, where we have to call on the imagination to help us express what we think needs to be said. We have entered the realm of spiritual myth and metaphor which it would be unintelligent of us to take literally – but which it would be even more stupid of us to ignore. That the victory of hope over death can only be expressed obliquely, colourfully, graphically, simply confirms the fact that there are occasions, not least to do with the transcendental openness of our humanity, on which we need to call on the imagination to tell some vital truth about ourselves. It is one of Catholicism's supreme strengths, so it seems to me, that it acknowledges and builds on this fact; and nowhere is this more true than in the accounts we have of the normative resurrection of Jesus from death and the tomb. There were no eye-witnesses to whatever it was that actually happened. But such accounts as we have unambiguously celebrate the triumph over the final demands of death which can be ours if we share the hope which undoubtedly inspired the human life of Jesus. There is no dodging death; but the resurrection of Jesus shows us that the very necessity of our future death, basic as it is to our experience of being human, can be so transformed as to be the way to living – now, in the present – that richer life of which our humanity is capable.

The blunt fact is that we do not actually know what occurs after death – not even whether the word 'occurs' would make any sense. Hope does not inform us of future facts – it enables us to face the far more important business of living a life defined by death. In matters concerning death, by far the best guide we have to our need to remember that in speaking in terms of a future life we are employing 'spiritual language' remains St Paul, quoting Isaiah, in a passage already quoted:

> ... as it is written,
> 'What no eye has seen, nor ear heard,
> nor the human heart conceived,
> what God has prepared for those who love him' –
> these things God has revealed to us through the Spirit ... And we speak of these things in words not taught by human wisdom but taught by the Spirit, interpreting spiritual things to those who are spiritual [or 'interpreting spiritual things in spiritual language'; or 'comparing spiritual things with spiritual'].
>
> (1 Corinthians 2:9f.,13 with NRSV variants;
> cf. Isaiah 64:4; 52:15)

We have come across the problem of what Paul may mean by 'spiritual' before; but I would say that a minimal meaning of the word – that is, one which does not invoke theological explanations which raise even more questions – is 'non-literal'; and it reminds us, once again, of the habitual mental reserve we need to maintain in the use of religious language, not only in matters surrounding our physically necessary deaths, but also in every other theological field as well.

Another necessity or imperative which, as I see it, belongs to the serious experience of being human concerns the human mind. In my experience of being human, I find an intellectual demand for a consciously truthful knowledge and understanding of oneself, of others, and of one's relationship to the world and its processes. What lies behind this unqualified, transcendental demand seems to me to be nothing other than the possession of mind and reason itself; simply because it is impossible to suppose that human faculties to do with knowing and understanding have any other purpose than the attainment of truth. Truthfulness is a transcendental quality of the human mind and reason – an absolute condition of their very possibility. If the human mind were not constitutively truth-seeking, it could not be other than pointless and void. Given the fact of our rational consciousness, it is surely an imperative necessity that we ensure that it is of the highest quality possible and attainable. This is not to say, of course, that we always manage to attain it; or even that we necessarily seek it in the right direction or for the right motives; or that numerous subjective and external influences do not distract and deflect us in our search. But the built-in orientation of mind and reason which was not towards truth would seem to be a plain nonsense – rather like a calculator that has been deliberately programmed to get its sums wrong. I would say that that experience of one's own humanity reveals an imperative orientation towards whatever kind of knowledge and understanding – whatever kind of truth – is appropriate and attainable in whatever field it is that one happens to be engaged.

The arts and the sciences have each their own hard-won brands of truth; and so, of course, has a religion like Catholicism. But it also appears that in humankind's imperative search for truthful knowledge and understanding, whether in the arts, the sciences – and not least in religion – there is an indispensable factor which is common to all. This factor I would be inclined, broadly speaking, to call a measure of trust, of imagination, perhaps even a kind of natural faith. However reflexively aware the efforts of a scholar or a scientist may be, however soundly based, critically controlled and coolly monitored their researches, there surely has to be, at least initially, an overall trust or faith in the imperative character of the search for the truth which fits the case. Otherwise it is difficult to see why or how the search could ever have got started, let alone have been continued. Again, conscious assumptions have to be made and maintained. Prior understandings – *Vorverständnisse* again – have to be openly acknowledged. Not everything is susceptible to being proved to bare reason's total satisfaction. No intelligent enquiry after truth begins – or can begin – straight from cold. What I am trying to suggest is that in all humankind's necessary search for truthful knowledge and understanding a constant and indispensable factor is what has been called 'a leap of faith' – a prior exercise of trust and imaginative insight. If this is correct, then it follows that it is far from alien to human beings to have the kind of faith in truth that I have tried to describe – indeed that it seems to be imperative for the fuller use of their inherent intelligence. I do not mean, of course, some specific religious faith as in the truth of Catholicism, but the kind of faith which consists in both a complete openness to the demands of the pursuit of truth, and a preparedness to make those leaps of the imagination (or faith) which will set the mind and the reason in motion and give them the boost and the support which they demand.

I would say that this need for imaginative openness, which seems to me to be an essential factor in the intellectual necessity which I think emerges from reflection on the experience of being human, is imposed on us by our simply being human; and it provides a thoroughly human basis for religious faith. The Catholic 'theological' virtue of faith thus emerges as one of the ways in which the constitutive human need and potential for faith can be satisfied – not to the limited degree afforded, entirely respectably, by the intellectual efforts demanded by this or that branch of the arts or sciences, but to the overall extent of the Catholic claim to offer salvation to the whole person. But as with the kind of human faith in truthful knowledge and understanding that befits the arts and sciences, so religious faith 'seeks understanding' for the human person, giving rise to an intellectual stance in which persons envision themselves, others and the world in terms of a religious pattern of meaning. It is about this religious faith-vision, its origin and its maintenance that more will be said later. For the moment my main concern is to stress that, far from running counter to anything that I can discern in the experience of being human, religious faith seems to correspond closely with the intellectual imperative that animates all humankind's efforts to achieve true knowledge and understanding. The grace and virtue of religious faith serves to bring out and activate a constituent factor in humanity; and so in its offer of religious faith Catholicism works towards our salvation.

A further necessity or imperative which I think is

discernible in personal reflection on the experience of being human is the demand that we must strive to achieve moral goodness in all we think and all we do. What constitutes moral goodness is a topic, of course, that would merit a complex debate and the thorough discussion of a number of theories of morality. But here I am speaking about what people commonly understand by their conscience, the power which they have ultimately to rely on to tell them what is morally good or evil. Conscience I take to be a rational faculty which monitors the moral quality of our lives and actions. That we possess moral consciences is what, I think, is clear from the experience of what it feels like to be human. There is imposed upon us a need for moral goodness. We refer our actions to rational norms. Conscience, in this sense, appears to be a transcendental human quality, in that it is an absolute condition of the possibility of being humanly good that we should be prepared to be called on to render a rational account of our actions. It would be impossible to think of being human without this imperative; and we regularly and rightly classify evil people who act immorally and show no sign of conscience as lacking humanity. But as with the mind's search for truthful knowledge and understanding where there are obstacles and distractions to be overcome, so with our rational search to be morally good. Immature or ill-informed or unexercised or insensitive consciences can succumb to the internal pressure of bad habits, and be misled, culpably and inculpably, by ignorance and sentimentality, and be lured off course by external influences and bogus rewards. It is also quite possible to suppress the imperative demands of conscience deliberately – with malice aforethought – and act with evil intent. To point these matters out is to be no more than realistic regarding the race to which we all belong.

That there exists in humankind a potential for moral evil which is so universally persistent that it can be said to be inherited is a view that Catholicism, picking up what the Bible says, has always embraced: '... all have sinned and fall short of the glory of God' (Romans 3:23). In Catholic theology this universal potential became traditionally known as 'original sin'. This important theologoumenon has been regularly misunderstood. It does not – either in the case of adults or of infants – have anything directly to do with the personal guilt or moral corruption which belong to what is called 'actual sin', mortal or venial; though it is no wonder that, confronted with the elaborate technicalities of 'moral theology' and its attendant casuistry, an observer of Catholicism might suppose that it is sometimes obsessed with the subject of sin. It has often been viewed as both over-emphasizing sin – and also as trivializing it. Yet Catholicism has contrived to be never less than realistic about sin. Sin, we must recall, is a theological metaphor, an 'offence against God', which expresses our human failure to respond to the demands of the moral necessity which conscience, one of the voices of necessity which we discern in the mystery of our existence, lays upon us. Failure is the central meaning of the bland Greek word used for 'sin' – *hamartia* – which means missing, failing to reach, or hit, our given targets. Moral realism has led Catholicism to give failure a certain prominence in its view of humankind; but an equivalent approach – though one which would have given far less scope to certain preachers – would have been to view the universal tendency to sin, not just in the negative light of moral failure, but in the positive light of a universal need for salvation. After all, what is sin but the dark side of the necessities to which we have not responded, as well as being a clear indication of our potential for being saved?

With equal realism, Catholicism stresses the difficulty we experience in following the demand to obey our consciences. It is not just that the demand is tough, or that we need to brace ourselves to face up to it with a certain stoic courage and determination. The difficulty we experience is that of actually overcoming the obstacles we discover within ourselves when we have to respond to the demand. Our habits help to build all sorts of blocks and barriers to our response – they are so embarrassingly familiar to us as to call for no description – but chief, and most serious, among these obstacles is surely that innate selfishness which makes us deliberately drag our moral heels, or turn a deaf ear or a blind eye, when we become aware of the demand of conscience. Here is a real obstacle to moral goodness which has to be positively surmounted, and Catholicism realistically acknowledges that we surmount our own selfishness only at a price. Response to the demands of our conscience is realistically seen as *costly*. It does not come easy to any of us. It calls for real self-sacrifice. It requires a surrender of all the works and pomps of the self combined with a positive embracing of the moral good in question. In other words, we need to be freely motivated by nothing less than *love*, if we are to achieve the moral goodness our experience of being human demands of us.

Hence Catholic theology has elaborated the moral need for grace, both 'actual' (to do with our actions) and 'sanctifying' (to do with our being in 'a state of grace'). But these, and further technicalities, may be left aside. The Catholic stress on grace is meant to provide an answer to the key question: where else might the spiritual help we plainly need to overcome our inner obstacles, and especially our selfishness, come from, if not from salvific contact with the saving mystery which defines us? Our moral need for grace is nothing other than a need for spiritual love, a need to love spiritually, and that need is fulfilled, provided we are open to it and willing to receive it, in our being graced by the divine Spirit who is the eternal love of the Son for the Father. In the metaphors of this high theology, our response to the moral imperative which we discern in our experience of being human – our becoming morally good – depends, not so much on ourselves (though our willing cooperation obviously needs to be evoked) as on the grace which is our way of sharing in the salvific mystery Catholics call the Trinity. Hence, too, Catholicism maintains an abiding interest in Mary and the saints, who serve as exemplars of the efficacy (complete in Mary's case) of divine grace, of love, over the obstacles our selfishness places in the path we have to follow in response to the demands of the imperative of conscience that we must be morally good.

༄

I trust I have made it sufficiently clear that my rough account of what I have called the necessities or imperatives – physical, intellectual and moral – which I claim to discern in my own experience of human existence is no more than a homespun attempt to give expression to how I personally imagine the situation to be. It has no professional pretence to scientific worth; indeed, in the circumstances, such pretence would simply obscure the matter. All the same, I cannot help being struck by the correspondence that has emerged between my three existential necessities and the three 'theological virtues' of hope, faith and love. I had never consciously foreseen, and so had not planned, any such correspondence. It would, of course, be easy to assign to it a greater importance than it may have; but since it has emerged, I intend to stick with it, since it will serve at least to illustrate an aspect of Catholicism which is key to understanding it as a religion – its view of the working relationship between what are traditionally called nature and grace. It amounts to one way of imagining how the salvation which Catholicism offers may be thought to work.

Catholicism imagines the spiritual grace which humankind needs for its salvation as nothing less or other than a participation in the life-giving mystery of the Trinity – a direct share in the divine Spirit, the mutual love of the Son and the Father, the three who, in the Catholic view, metaphorically encapsulate and express the new meaning of God which Catholicism promotes. Grace is, far too often, thought of as a commodity which God freely dispenses, and which we accept, so that we are kept in 'a state of grace' or are helped to perform some good action or to persevere in goodness; or which we reject, so that we find ourselves 'living in sin', or falling into committing sins – and so forth. Perhaps these homely notions of grace may have their uses; but they mask the key idea that grace is a metaphor for what may perhaps be described as the 'godliness', the holiness, that is demanded of us – that participation in the mystery we call the Trinity, which we need, not only to overcome our various failures to meet the transcendental demands of our own humanity, but also to heal our tendencies to fail, and at the same time to enable us to become the persons we are capable of being. This paradox – that humankind is such that at the deepest level it calls for empowerment from a source which is always greater than itself to save it and make it what it has only the damaged potential to become (*Deus semper maior*) – is a basic principle of Catholicism and the root of the Catholic metaphor of divine grace and salvation. Behind the paradox lies the fact that it is only in a sharing in its own mystery (call it God or Trinity) which takes it out of itself that humankind can be 'justified', fundamentally 'ad-justed', and thereby saved to become its real self. We have already seen how the Council of Trent described the process of justification – a person's passage from a state of sin into a state of grace. The paragraph quoted above (p. 74f.) includes so much that is key to the Catholic view of salvation as a generous impartation of God's own Spirit of love which integrates itself with the life of the recipient, thereby eliminating sin and spiritually endowing the person with the identity of Christ through the gifts of his faith, hope and love. More will be said later about the pivotal matter of our 'incorporation' into Christ.

But for the moment, I want to stay with what is said about faith, hope and love – the 'theological virtues' which turned out to correspond so closely with the transcendental necessities of human existence as I claim to experience them. I do this because, it will be recalled, I set out to enquire about how Catholicism may be thought to work as a religion; and I consider that it is faith, hope and love that adequately define the modes in which Catholic spirituality is meant to work for our salvation in our earthbound situation. Open to the mystery of our humanity, we are endowed with the Spirit which enables us to cope with the necessity of death and to *hope* in the transforming consummation of our lives; which enables us to attend responsibly to the truth of things and to keep *faith* with an elected view of our world as seen in the light of God; and which enables us to respond to the call to goodness with the self-sacrificing *love* by which our morality moves into the realm of the very holiness of the Spirit whereby the Son loves the Father. In other words, the working of Catholicism does not so much alter, or just add to, the ordinary lives we all have to lead as radically transform them, insofar as our whole response to the necessities of human living is now animated by hope, faith and love.

I make no apology for repeating a passage I quoted from from St Paul (p. 74). For him, faith, hope and love belonged indissolubly to the salvific efficacity of the religion he preached:

> Therefore, since we are justified by *faith*, we have peace with God through our Lord Jesus Christ, through whom we have obtained access to this grace in which we stand; and we boast in our *hope* of sharing the glory of God. And not only that, but we also boast in our sufferings, knowing that sufferings produce endurance, and endurance produces character, and character produces *hope*, and *hope* does not disappoint us, because God's *love* has been poured into our hearts through the Holy Spirit that has been given to us.
> (Romans 5:1–5, my italics)

This is no merely theological reflection on the human condition, but the reported experience of what it is like to be human in the light of Christ, and how the spiritual religion which Paul did so much to develop worked in addressing the needs – the necessities, the imperatives, the demands – which the experience of being human manifests. So it comes as no surprise that when he sang the praises of the 'still more excellent way', he severely sidelined the more eye-catching religious manifestations of speaking in tongues and prophesying and understanding 'all mysteries and all knowledge' and wonder-working and extreme self-denial, in favour of giving clear priority to the primacy of love, with its attendant faith and hope. Love

> does not rejoice in wrongdoing, but rejoices in the truth. It bears all things, believes all things, hopes all things, endures all things ... Love never ends. (1 Corinthians 13:6–8)

whereas prophecy and esoteric knowledge are only ever partial, are doomed to come to an end and are to be associated with religious immaturity.

> For now we see in a mirror, dimly [or 'in a riddle'], but then we will see face to face. Now I know only in part; then I will know fully, even as I have been fully known. And now faith,

hope, and love abide, these three; and the greatest of these is love. (1 Corinthians 13:12f)

The most striking quality in this familiar passage is, I think, its clear emphasis on ordinariness – its conviction that the Corinthians should grow, like Paul, out of their spiritual adolescence and its exotic but puerile and transient displays of spiritual power, and learn to live, before all else, ordinary, demanding, prosaic, quotidian lives in the power of faith, hope and love, with love rendering hope and faith effective – 'the only thing that counts is faith working [or, made effective] through love' (Galatians 5:6). The 'theological virtues' of Catholicism point out the same truth – that salvation does not consist in expecting to be able to see or to know or to be able to describe our ultimate mystery or our eventual fate. What the necessary virtues of faith, hope and love furnish us with is the ability to respond in an ordinary and realistic way to the demands of daily human living. All three take us out of our deficient selves, not by plucking us from the ordinary mass of humankind and transplanting us into a world apart, but by enabling us to live responsible and responsive human lives wherever we happen to be – responsible for our own mystery-defined humanity, and responsive to its demands and to the demands of the humanity of others. The God to whom Catholics are meant to respond might be best re-imagined as a God whose mystery reveals itself, not so much as *existing* apart from ourselves, as *insisting* from the depths of our own humanity that the demands which constitute the fabric of that humanity are duly met, and a God who constantly offers us the power of his own Spirit within us to help us to meet them. Such is the religious vision of humanity which is that of Catholicism. It is in appropriating this Catholic vision of humanity that our spiritual salvation comes to be wrought.

❦

But it is no abstract vision based on some ephemeral hunch regarding the existential experience of being human. The Catholic vision of humanity retains its evangelical source in Jesus as the man whose experience of human existence and of the whole mystery which surrounds our being human was found to be so intensely and uniquely definitive that theological interpretation could not rest until it had declared, once and for all, that Jesus was God in person – incarnate God, the divine Son whose ordinary humanity functioned with such responsiveness to its own mystery that Jesus was understood to share personally in that mystery, and so to take his place in the salvific economy of the Trinity 'for us and for our salvation'. With the theologoumenon of the Trinity we must now associate the theologoumenon of the Incarnation, in terms of which the fullness of the humanity we have in common with Jesus is swept by the power of the Spirit into Jesus' own relatedness as Son to the Father. Both doctrines, Trinity and Incarnation, are absolutely indispensable to a proper understanding of the way Catholicism works – taken together both doctrines provide the theological model of Catholicism as a salvation religion. Without some effective knowledge of them both, Catholicism is reduced to a nondescript distortion of itself, bereft of the distinctiveness which makes it the religion it actually is, and, more importantly, lacking those imaginatively powerful religious features which reveal the way of Catholic salvation.

Fortunately, in the case of the Incarnation there exists (as there does not for the doctrine of the Trinity) an officially formulated theological 'Definition' which unsurpassably expresses what several generations of theologians had eventually come to understand by the doctrine. At the Fourth Ecumenical Council of the Church, held at Chalcedon (near Istanbul) in AD 451, the assembled Fathers not only formally re-issued and endorsed the all-important creeds of the earlier Councils of Nicaea (325) and Constantinople (381) and other canonical texts from churches of the West and the East; they also drafted a masterly summary or 'Definition' of the Catholic doctrine of the Incarnation. Acute controversy over the correct theological interpretation of Jesus had dogged the Church's thought and mission from the start. The Council of Chalcedon hoped to bring the controversy to an end – the kind of hope which, sadly, no Church Council ever sees fulfilled – by devising a formulary that would satisfy the disputing parties once and for all. The operative summary which the Council agreed and issued is arguably the prime artefact, the noblest theologoumenon, of the Catholic doctrinal tradition. Quoting it is unavoidable, so I make no apology for presenting this tough text which, as I see it, is absolutely fundamental to the understanding of Catholicism as a means of human salvation.

> Following then the holy Fathers, we confess that our Lord Jesus Christ is a single identical ['one and the same'] Son, and all of us agree with one another in teaching that he is complete in divinity and that he is complete in humanity; truly God and truly a human being; that he has a rational soul and a body; that in his divinity he is of the same being as the Father, and that in his humanity he is of the same being as we are, in every way like us except for sin [Hebrews 4:15]; that before the ages he was begotten in his divinity from the Father; but that in the last days, for us and for our salvation, in his humanity from Mary the Virgin Mother of God – a single identical Christ, Son, Lord, Only-begotten, acknowledged as being in two natures with no confusion, change, distinction or division; that at no point has the difference between the natures been destroyed through the union, but the characteristics of each nature are all the better preserved and meet up in a single person and a single reality; that he is not parted or divided into two persons, but that there is a single identical Son and Only-begotten God, Word, Lord, Jesus Christ, just as the prophets and the Lord Jesus Christ himself taught us concerning him, and the creed of the Fathers handed it down to us.
> (Greek text in Denzinger-Schönmetzer, ##301–2, my translation)

What is immediately striking is that the Council chose to express itself in a brilliant collage of technical theologoumena in which what is said of the divinity of Jesus (complete, true, full, begotten) is exactly balanced in words by what is said of his humanity (complete, true, full, born). It is from this interpretation of Jesus that there emerges the further theologoumenon of there being two natures united in his single, identical person. The union of the two natures – Alexandrian theologians referred to it as 'the hypostatic [roughly, 'real and personal'] union' – left both natures exactly as they were. They did not fuse with one another, nor alter one another through their union, nor did they distance or separate themselves from one another in any way. Far from creating problems with either nature, their union simply brought the best out in both, as they met in the single, identical person of Jesus. Of course, this supreme example of the theologian's craft deserves much more detailed commentary than can be given here; and it needs above all to be carefully explained against the background of the acute Christological controversies of the fourth and fifth centuries. But I want simply to point out three matters of key importance.

First, the Chalcedonian Definition is a highly wrought and polished piece of theology which was meant to provide a technical formula to which various schools of Christological thought could be invited to subscribe. It also had a political purpose in that it was striving to bring together patriarchates whose mutual hostility included significantly different approaches to the theological interpretation of Jesus. Hence the immense care expended on the rhetorical balance of the phrases which express the theological duality (the two natures) of Jesus, and on the highly emphatic repetition of the fact of their unity in his single, identical person. Nothing is to compromise the theological duality, and nothing is to diminish the concrete unity of his person. Jesus is not just anybody, just another man, nor some god posing as a man, nor a manlike pantomime horse, with two components loosely conjoined and occasionally cooperating inside. The Chalcedonian Jesus represents Jesus as interpreted in theological terms which are reaching for the heights of acceptable theological correctness without in the least compromising the utter reality of his evangelical reality. But we must carefully note that 'two natures in one person' in no way represents a factual description of how actually Jesus experienced the mystery of his own human existence. Failure to grasp the elementary point that we are dealing here with a sophisticated theologoumenon, and not any kind of physical or psychological description of Jesus, has caused an endless waste of theologians' time and effort, as they have tried to reconcile the presence and activity of divinity (about which they had no direct knowledge) with Jesus' obvious humanity.

Second, it is in any case ridiculous to suppose that any such reconciliation is at all feasible. The theological model of 'two natures in one person' cannot be taken literally or factually, if only because, in the case of 'divine nature' we cannot know what we are talking about. All we can know is that 'divine nature', however we may attempt to conceive it, can never be commensurate, let alone literally reconcilable, with what we know of 'human nature', since the former must infinitely transcend the latter in every possible way. Divinity and humanity are not two comparable commodities. In other words, in speaking of 'two natures in one person' we are involving ourselves in imaginative theological interpretation – with pure theologoumena. Not that Jesus himself, as a real, concrete human being, is any sort of theologoumenon. What Chalcedon does is to lay it down that, if we wish to interpret and understand Jesus in theologoumenal terms, we shall need to speak of him as being one person with two natures. To speak so is to maintain proper religious orthodoxy. But we should always remember what it is that we are doing. We are not describing Jesus' make-up – we are trying, clumsily, to get our human minds round his importance and his function by the use of theological terms.

Third, the overall purpose of Chalcedon's theological interpretation of Jesus is to provide acceptably orthodox theological terminology whereby we are enabled, bearing in mind the limitations of our human understanding, to keep our thinking about the meaning and function of Jesus as our Saviour on the right lines. In other words, despite all the technically sophisticated theology which Chalcedon found it necessary to employ in its Definition, the Council's purpose has as much to do with Jesus' work 'for us and for our salvation' as have the earlier creeds which the Council was so careful to endorse. Our salvation depends absolutely, says the Council, on the sheer, concrete unity of Jesus – the factual, historical integrity of the human being which he undoubtedly was. If we are to understand this man properly in his function as our Saviour, we need to interpret him in theological terms as everything we can possibly mean by 'God' (his divinity), whilst maintaining him to be everything we normally mean by 'man' (his humanity). In an aside, the Council notes that Jesus' sinlessness, while setting him apart from sinners like ourselves, in no way diminishes the humanity we all share. Humanity was never meant to be sinful, and sin, far from being an essential part of being human, indicates the presence of a deficiency in humanity. So Jesus saves us in a wholly new and specific way – by being a real, sinless man, whose complete humanity uniquely exists in and through the spiritual union of a perfect Son with the God he calls 'Father'. At this point the Catholic doctrines of the incarnation and the Trinity combine to achieve their salvific purpose.

It would be wrong not to remark on the difference between this understanding of Chalcedon and the way in which it has been commonly understood. It is perhaps forgivable that, given what appears to be the active presence of two natures in Jesus, it has been to his theologoumenal divinity that the work of our salvation has become wholly attributed. It has seemed only right that religious reverence and piety should demand that this is the case. Surely, since salvation is the work of God, it is only in virtue of being divine that Jesus can save. But this is precisely to miss *the whole point* of what Catholic and Chalcedonian orthodoxy declares. In other religions it may be the case that only gods themselves can save. In Chalcedonian Catholicism – and this, I believe, is precisely what sets Catholicism quite apart from all other religions, or at least puts Catholicism into a religious class of its own – it is the humanity of Jesus (complete, true, full, born) in personal solidarity with the divinity which his followers were rightly inspired to see in him which is the actual, operative principle of our salvation. Jesus is, first and foremost and definitively, a *human* saviour. It is precisely the common humanity which is personally and uniquely his that constitutes him as our saviour. Jesus' humanity is not a minor or secondary accessory or appendage to his divinity. His divinity, being true, full, complete and begotten, cannot possibly be regarded as another associated element or factor in a composite make-up; and Chalcedon goes to great lengths to say that this is not the case. He was emphatically not (in the notorious words of a certain distinguished preacher) 'half man, half God'.

Another way of appreciating this key move on the part of Chalcedon would be to view the Council as working out its formulary on two distinct levels of thought: on the level of the absolute unity, the actual, concrete, integral oneness of Jesus, and on the different level of his theologically abstract duality, the theologoumenal level of his two natures. The Council, very wisely, makes no attempt to reconcile these two levels of unity and duality, precisely because the two levels do not speak the same kind of language. One level is speaking of Jesus as the real human being that he undoubtedly was. The other level is the level at which that real human being is being theologically interpreted with a view to his being properly understood and appreciated within the logic of the Catholic religion. The levels of reality and of its theological interpretation are kept quite distinct. Jesus is not being thought of as both single and dual at some same level. If such were the case, he would emerge as a monstrosity, incapable of the human life and death of which we read in the Gospels. Chalcedon was doing theology. It was spelling out the terms which it thought should structure the theological understanding of Jesus, if it were to be counted orthodox. It was not trying to describe what Jesus was actually like. It was devising rules for the orthodox theological understanding of the meaning of Jesus as our Saviour. It was in effect declaring: whatever you think and say about Jesus, make sure that you think and say that he personally shares so truly and fully and uniquely in the mystery of his humanity which he called Father, that it is right to predicate of him all the attributes that belong to his being that Father's divine Son; and also make sure that you think and say nothing that would detract in any way (not even given that he was sinless) from his being just as human as we are. Far from describing what Jesus was actually like, Chalcedon was giving us the paradigm of the theological grammar for thinking and speaking about Jesus in an orthodox fashion. They are rules that remain in force today for Catholicism's understanding of its Saviour.

Jesus, in Chalcedonian terms, was a human being who had such unitary concreteness as we all enjoy – he was simply 'a single person and a single reality'. His humanity, in all its human actions, served as the revelatory agent which declares him, for those who have faith in him, to be divine. It is through his humanity that he becomes their God and their Saviour. In human terms (which are the only terms we have at our disposal), it is what his followers acknowledged to be a new and unique human insight into the mystery of his own, and our common, human existence, expressed in so many ways in word and action in the Gospels, that led them to acknowledge his divinity. That Jesus himself was aware, however hesitatingly, of his own personal status and function may seem probable from our reading of the Gospels, but we must remember that they were written to give precisely this impression. That he directly claimed divinity for himself is both highly unlikely in itself, and hardly sustained even by the Gospel evidence. We must be very careful to treat Jesus' divinity, not as a quality or a commodity, but, in the only way open to us, as a theologoumenon, as an appropriate and necessary interpretation of Jesus' person in terms of God. And in trying to understand his person and his function in terms of Chalcedonian orthodoxy, it is especially crucial not to put the theologoumenal cart of his divinity before the actual horse of his unique and perfect humanity, which is what, I believe, gives the salvation offered by the religion of Catholicism its defining uniqueness.

⁕

What I am trying to establish is that Chalcedonian and Catholic orthodoxy licenses the kind of approach I have been making to the salvific function played by Jesus the man, through his human faith, hope and love, We are saved by sharing in his Spirit, through those human graces which Jesus himself displayed in his life and death. They are the graces whereby he responded, in his unique way, to the mystery of his own human existence, to the demands and necessities of that human existence as he experienced it. They are the graces which brought him to that fulfilment of his humanity which was wrought in the way he lived, suffered and died on the Cross, and which was crowned in his achievement of human glory in what was understood to be his resurrection from the dead. They are the graces which invite us to share his spiritual insight into the reality of the world in which human beings are to lead their lives, die their deaths, and achieve the fulfilment which is properly theirs. In order to support us in being able to do this, generations of theologians have constructed and articulated the Catholic vision of reality which is offered to us in the system of beliefs which is expressed in the Catholic creeds and the doctrinal tradition of the Church.

The religion of Catholicism, therefore, and the salvation which it offers, comes down to being a matter of sharing a certain vision – 'a vision thing', as it might be called these days. It is an imaginative vision created out of the theological metaphors it chooses to employ – a meaningful vision which, insofar as it is not literally descriptive of the world we have to live in, is projected on to that world. Theology does this for religious and spiritual purposes. The construction and creation of the theological world is not a matter of probing the unknown in order to satisfy the curiosity. It is a matter of endowing the actual world in which we have to live with a religious meaning and a religious truth through the creative imagining of its religious dimensions, dimensions which will make living in this world, with all its physical, intellectual and moral demands, manageable and fulfilling. It is in this way – and not by satisfying our curiosity about some other literally describable world – that theology makes its contribution towards our salvation. It supposes that without an imaginatively articulated religious vision, humankind would remain severely impoverished and even retarded.

What the Catholic vision does is to locate humankind and the mystery which envelops it within an imaginatively articulated and intelligible picture of a world which is systematically organized round the supreme metaphor of a God and his actions. Not, of course, that treating God as a supreme metaphor has anything to do with a denial of the essentially saving mystery of what 'God', in our limited way of thinking and speaking, has to stand for. On the contrary, to treat 'God' as a metaphor is the only way we have of ensuring that the whole mystery of our salvation is rigorously preserved, and does not become idolatrously objectivised. The systematically theological presentation of the Catholic vision results from centuries of elaboration and development by creative human minds and imaginations as they searched for appropriate materials through which to express the vision coherently, intelligibly and effectively for the religious requirements of their own tradition of the faith, hope and love of Jesus.

Perhaps the element in the Catholic tradition which might best exemplify the theological process of the imaginative assimilation of already existing materials into the expression of the new salvific vision of the world which Catholicism had to offer lies in its view of the world's creation. It is well known that other religions, not least Judaism, and many philosophies, especially those which were influenced by Platonism, had their views of how the world might be thought to have come into existence. There was certainly no shortage of creation materials for Catholicism to utilize in constructing its own view, important as this was for the theological account of the vision of reality which Catholicism wished to promote. None of the pre-existing materials would fit this vision, and all would need radical adaptation if the novelty and spiritual force of the vision was to be properly expressed. The vision had to be, not just theocentric, but above all else, Christocentric, since it was a vision in which the whole of reality, from its very beginnings to whatever might be its end, was structured and formed as the unified field in which Christ would be seen as active from start to finish as the saviour of humankind. So known materials had to be imaginatively selected and adapted and expanded until the whole world's creation in Christ became expressible, with Christ, as the Father's Word, playing his full part along with the creative Spirit in the very founding of reality; and in such a formative way that the whole of reality would find its salvation, and eventually its completion, in and through him alone. Such was the imaginative vision of the creation of reality which Catholic theology discovers in its earliest sources.

It is a matter of theological, imaginative religious vision, of course, and not of scientific theory and hypothesis. However fascinating one may find the latest cosmological theories presented by contemporary science, beautiful and even terrible as they are, they have, of course, nothing directly to do with the salvific workings of a spiritual religion. They certainly arouse awe and wonder, and rightly, but apart from prompting vivid images of unthinkable space and time, of elemental violence and immeasurable distances, they can add nothing to the imaginative spiritual vision of reality which has its beginnings in the Catholic view of creation. For this reason, I find it hard to see any point in the kind of arguments that characterize the efforts of those who either try to reconcile religion and science, or who are determined to keep them firmly apart, usually as a way of showing how inferior religion is to science. To my mind, these efforts rest on a simple mistake: namely that of supposing that they have anything in common to start with. Whereas science builds its picture of reality through observation and rigorous experiment, a spiritual religion constructs its vision of reality on its own imaginative interpretation of it in the light of the mystery of humankind's experienced need for salvation from its very beginning. The religious doctrine of creation serves to maintain the overall scope of the vision of reality involved in the Catholic doctrine of salvation.

⁕

The maintenance of the Catholic vision prompts reflection on the part which prayer plays in Catholic life. In a true sense the continuous sharing of the faith-vision of Jesus on the part of a Catholic is in itself the chief act of personal prayer. St Paul, we must recall, encouraged his converts to 'Rejoice always, pray without ceasing [*adialeiptôs* – leaving no gaps or intervals], give thanks in all circumstances ...'

(1 Thessalonians 5:16–18); and perhaps what he meant was the positive acceptance of the new vision which belongs to the faith of Jesus, and the steady attention that needs to be given to it. Prayer, in its many forms, is rightly given pride of place among religious acts, and this is certainly the case in Catholicism. If Catholicism is above all else a matter of sharing the vision of reality which is to be discerned in the human faith of Jesus, then personal prayer is the religious activity or exercise whose purpose is to maintain, to deepen and to enlarge our share in that vision. 'The raising up of the mind and heart to God' is the definition of prayer that most Catholics will have learnt from the days when they had to learn the Catechism by heart. The Catechism contained few more accurate definitions. Less helpful, perhaps, was the perfunctory way in which the activity of prayer was explained. It was generally assumed that personal prayer was predominantly a matter of regularly reciting certain given prayer formulas or of involving oneself in certain devotional exercises, often on getting out of bed in the morning or getting back into it at night. There is, of course, nothing at all objectionable in such exercises; and the promotion of the regular and habitual practice of them can only be good. But I think it is fair to say that very little was taught about the deeper purpose of personal prayer, and still less about how essential it is to the faith-vision, the sharing of which is basic to being a Catholic.

In other words, compared with the kind of personal prayer that should be expected in a mature Catholic, what most have learnt about prayer in their past generally remains mechanical and superficial. In line with the view of Catholicism I have been developing in this essay, I need to suggest a broader and deeper approach to personal prayer which is directly linked with the way in which I see Catholicism working. I do not think personal prayer is primarily to do with technique or method, although I would be far from discouraging anyone from using whatever technique or method helps their personal engagement in prayer in whatever situation they find themselves. I have to confess that, for myself, techniques and methods which I have not thought out for myself have long proved useless – except to distract me from the way I find I need to pray anyway. But I am no example for anyone, and I have no practical suggestions of a general nature to offer. This is because I maintain that prayer is, at root, a personal involvement in one's own mode of Catholicism, one's own way of understanding what it is to be a Catholic. So praying will be as various as the ways in which people hold to their Catholicism. All the same, I think it may be helpful to suggest, very briefly, how personal prayer might make use of the two levels of faith and belief which, as I have suggested, are helpful in dealing with Catholicism.

The primary level at which personal prayer is essential for the mature Catholic is at the level of the human faith, hope and love of Jesus. That is, prayer is a conscious participation in his total commitment to the mystery of his personal humanity which he addressed as Father. As such it involves attitudes of worship and adoration, of devotion and commitment. I have mentioned the Catechism definition of prayer as 'the raising up of the mind and heart to God', and this is a precise description of what is meant here. In the power of Jesus' personal Spirit, we attentively appropriate our own personal experience of being human, become conscious of the ways in which we might have fallen short of humanity's demands, and raise our human minds and hearts to what we discern as their own defining mystery (which we call God). Alternative to speaking of raising our minds and hearts to that mystery, we might speak of plunging them into its mysterious depths, 'for the Spirit searches everything, even the depths of God' (1 Corinthians 2:10). Raising or plunging, it matters little – there is no escaping the metaphorical density of the language about prayer at this primary level of shared faith, hope and love in face of the mystery of God. With the human faith, hope and love of Jesus himself we set ourselves to discerning and assimilating the defining mystery of our common humanity.

At this level, praying must be more than the occasional performance of some ephemeral exercise. It is more accurate to speak of a *state* of prayer than of an act of prayer, since at its best this level of prayer would involve a potentially permanent consciousness of faith, hope and love as orientations of the self towards Jesus and the acquisition of his mind-set. It could be properly called contemplative, since it consists of a long and steady awareness of the mystery which defines us as we respond to it in faith, hope and love. More accurately still, the practice of this level of prayer is meant to become mystically transformative of ourselves into the image of Jesus himself in his glory as we take on his vision and his values. I have stressed from the start that I do not think of God as an objective entity whom we have to confront in prayer; and I have also suggested that Catholicism is a basically mystical religion, essentially focused on the mystery revealed in our own humanity as shared with that of Jesus. Hence it cannot be surprising that I see prayer at this primary level as the personal exercising of the mystical qualities involved in being a Catholic. I cannot say that this view receives much support from official church teachings or attitudes, but from my experience I remain fairly sure that, in their own far simpler and far better way, many good Catholics do rise to this level of prayer in much this way. Two brief quotations from St Paul might repay careful pondering at this point. With due respect to other translations, I present them in my own version:

> It is whenever [Moses] turns to the Lord that the veil is removed [Exodus 34:34]. But the Lord is the Spirit, and where there is the Lord's Spirit, there is freedom. It is with unveiled faces that we are all reflecting the Lord's glory, and are being transformed into its very likeness from one degree of glory to the next, such is the effect of the Lord who is Spirit.
> (2 Corinthians 3:16–18; cf. Exodus 34:33–35)

> The country we belong to exists in heaven, and it is from there that we are eagerly awaiting a Saviour, the Lord Jesus Christ. He will transfigure the bodies which humiliate us and conform them, through the operation of his power to subject everything to himself, to the body which is his in glory.
> (Philippians 3:20–21)

Nothing, to my mind, better describes the steady stance and the hoped-for outcome of personal prayer at what I have called the primary level of faith.

But there is also a secondary, more formal level at which the Catholic needs to pray, the level at which personal prayer is more of an exercise at the level of the beliefs of the Catholic tradition. This is the level, not of transformative union with Jesus in sharing the faith, hope and love which fill his mind and heart, but of acquiring his faith-vision of the world and of learning to act in accordance with it. It is at this level that Catholics appropriate, learn to make their own, the vision that the theologoumenal beliefs of Catholicism have been imaginatively constructed to shape and to structure. And just as faith and beliefs are both separate and radically interdependent, so also the primary and secondary levels of prayer, whilst they are different, service one another, prayer at the primary level of faith constantly attending to the kind of spiritual understanding of reality which is vividly and dramatically supplied by the Catholic system of beliefs. At this secondary level personal prayer might consist in a positive acceptance of that spiritual vision of reality as embracing oneself, one's fellow-human beings, and the whole world and its affairs in general. In the light of this religious vision petitionary prayer would have its place, in the sense of a fervently expressed hope and desire that what has or might still come about would conform with requirements of the vision as a whole. Prayer for the living and the dead would seek to locate them all within the scope of that vision of reality which Catholic beliefs provide.

But what of the more obvious Catholic practice of 'saying your prayers'? The question was important enough from the beginning to merit consideration in Matthew's 'Sermon on the Mount'. Great emphasis is laid on praying – as on giving alms – in privacy, even in secrecy; and as for the manner of praying,

> '... When you are praying, do not heap up empty phrases as the Gentiles do; for they think they will be heard because of their many words. Do not be like them, for your Father knows what you need before you ask him. Pray then in this way ...' [and there follows the Our Father]. (Matthew 6:7–9)

We can only suppose that the Our Father, even in Matthew's longer version, 6:9–13 (Luke's version is only half as long, 11:2–4) is meant to serve as a model of the terms in which personal and private prayer is to be made, as well as being an example of how to be economical with words in prayer. Words, as we have constantly discovered in the course of this book, are both indispensable and also out of their depth when it comes to coping with the spiritual meaning of Catholicism, and perhaps especially in the kind of personal prayer I have tried to describe above. Whilst their use is certainly licensed, and in fact recommended, they need to be used with caution, giving such support as is necessary to the two levels of personal prayer I have tried to describe above, and without usurping the strictly spiritual processes involved in such prayer.

The choice of prayers and words which are suitable for personal prayer is, in my view, wide enough to satisfy most of the purposes such prayer might have, although some personal tastes will no doubt call on other sources as well. It is obvious that the Our Father itself will be the standard and basic source for Catholic personal prayer, providing, as it claims to do, a comprehensive account of the way Jesus himself prayed, and giving unique access to the issues and the petitions which his human mind and heart found it necessary to express in prayer to the one he addressed as Father. We can never hope to do better than share in Jesus's own personal devotion to what he referred to as the Name, the Kingdom and the Will of the Father, abiding aspects of the mystery he discerned in his own humanity. Nor, given the earthly focus of ordinary daily life and the constant necessities to which we and others have to respond, might we dispense with being permanent petitioners for the fulfilment of all our daily requirements. Our forgiveness of others as a strict condition for the overlooking of our own shortcomings lies at the very heart of a spirituality which involves the transcending of our inherent selfishness and our transformation into a mystical identification with one who consistently taught his followers to love their enemies, and who himself forgave his killers even as he died. The

Our Father makes dramatically clear the costliness of our new life in the Spirit of Jesus, and it is entirely realistic in ensuring that we pray that we will be spared being tested beyond our strength, and freed from being held back by the grip of evil.

A further key source is surely the Book of Psalms, so broad in its appeal, so varied in its moods, and so powerful and direct in its effect, not least when the Psalms are prayed or recited in a Catholic context as expressions of Jesus' own praying mind and heart. It is not difficult to see why the community of Jesus' followers, no doubt inspired by his own use of the Psalms in prayer and by familiar Jewish usage, eventually developed the practice of organizing their daily prayer so that it brought the whole day into the ambit of their prayer. Thus organized into the several daily sections of what is known as 'the Divine Office' – the performance of the duty of prayer – the Psalms have for centuries helped to provide that continuity in personal prayer which a mature Catholicism requires. The same might be said of the contemplative use of the Rosary or of other standard Catholic devotions. Catholicism has long encouraged continuous personal prayer to support the spiritual attitude in face of reality which its visionary faith and its supporting beliefs require. Prayer sets the measure of our willingness to cooperate in the spiritual work of our salvation.

Chapter 5

Church

There can be no adequate consideration of the spiritual functioning of Catholicism without some proper consideration of the part played in it by the Catholic Church. I shall consider the Church in the light of the view of Catholicism which I have been suggesting. It seems to me that it is only when there has been some coherent attempt at understanding the ways in which the religion and spirituality of Catholicism are meant to work that it is possible to give intelligent consideration to the ways in which the Church might be expected to exercise such responsibilities as it has with regard to that religion. There can be little doubt that there are signs of a popular, possibly growing, view among Catholics – not to mention others – that the institutional Church can represent a serious deterrent to the embracing of what are sensed to be the religious and spiritual ideals and principles of Catholicism. At any rate, it is quite common to come across people in many walks of life who have enjoyed, and even appreciated, the benefits of a Catholic upbringing and education, only to abandon the practice of their religion at the earliest adult opportunity. So often their problem is not so much with their Catholicism – or with what they have been led to think of as their Catholicism – as with the institutionalized manner in which it is presented to them. There are also many in other Christian Churches who hold much the same view about how those Churches represent the form of Christianity they favour. Was it not a senior Anglican clergyman who unforgettably remarked, many years ago: 'Thank goodness for the Church – it is the only thing that stands between us and God'?

Again, apart from personal reactions, other public fads

militate against the institutional Church and its seemingly clumsy or ill-judged efforts to remain unworldly in a distinctly worldly age – an age where in so many of the world's institutions the leading values that count are cheap and shallow; where fame and celebrity are constantly encouraged to the detriment of the solid ordinary goodness of human persons; where the advertising of rubbishy products constantly boosts consumerism and lowers taste; where any sense of personal depth and mystery is largely lost or is faddishly pursued in the wrong direction in a multitude of patently bogus ways; where personal responsibility is routinely shifted elsewhere; where so little is ever thought through to its conclusions; where so much energy is expended on reaching fake goals or establishing what the wise have known for centuries, or on setting false targets and on being cost-efficient – whilst all the while dabbling in the quasi-religion of 'mission statements' and superficial corporate mystique. Not that I consider it is a bad world to live in. Wonderful things are constantly achieved despite institutions, and sometimes even by them. But perhaps because of their ceaseless self-advertisement, not to mention their routinely exaggerated and often transparently dishonest claims, people are increasingly invited to judge all public institutions, including those with which they may have no connection, by the generally corrupt ways in which so many institutions seek to fulfil their declared purposes. People have had to become more sophisticated in their judgements. Perceived failures are severely censured, and success and value for money are expected. There is widespread critical awareness of whether institutions are performing or not. However unsound popular standards may be, similar criteria are commonly applied to the Churches, and not least to the institutional Catholic Church, which still seems to present an obvious target which looms surprisingly large on people's horizons, at least on occasions. A scandal, the death of a Pope, the election of his successor – all these, and many other matters, keep the institutional Church well in the public eye. But by what criteria should its performance really be judged? By what criteria should it be prepared, when called on, to adapt that performance to the requirements of a critical age? I would say that there are two criteria by which the institutional Roman Church should be judged, and both of them are directly related to its spiritual mission. Its mission should be uncompromisingly *evangelical*, and its mode of operation in fulfilling this mission in the world should be *sacramental*.

☙

I begin by taking the Catholic Church in the straightforward sense of the institutional and hierarchically organized gathering (*ekklesia*) of all those whose faith in God involves the acceptance of the discipline and the practices, as well as the profession of the theological beliefs, developed by the orthodox Catholic tradition. The Catholic Church, in this sense and as I happen to know it, is centred on Rome, from where it has exercised largely uninterrupted responsibility for the spiritual functioning of Catholicism. Roman Catholicism I take to be, despite what some might consider undesirable or unnecessary developments, still the least inauthentic form of Christianity on offer in the West. This may sound an ungenerous remark, hardly in keeping with my display of personal confidence in the way Catholicism may be interpreted as an effective, working human spirituality. But it is prompted by the limited extent to which the Church and its mission can be said to have been consistently inspired by evangelical values. It is plain to see that the Roman Church did not become the institution it has become solely by conforming to the demands of the Gospel; and that it has from time to time vigorously pursued worldly values which openly contradict the spiritual teachings of Jesus. There is no point in arguing about this. Protestant reform movements in many periods of the Church's history had right on their side when they realized that the Church was not measuring up to its evangelical nature. How those movements went about attempting to reform the Church, and what was lost in the attempt is another matter. Schism and heresy could hardly be expected to be of much use, although perhaps little else was possible at the time. But the application of the evangelical criterion to the Church and its mission needs handling with care. It cannot be simplistically applied to the Church, since such an application would ignore two thousand years of developing interpretation and intelligent understanding, all closely historically conditioned, of the values and the vision of the New Testament. Nonetheless the evangelical criterion will hardly admit of compromise; and it remains right to demand that the institutional Church's performance of its spiritual mission be judged by it. Maintaining its true base in the original inspiration of Catholicism is an overriding priority for the Church. It belongs to my own emphasis on the unbroken inspiration which Catholicism itself must derive from the faith, hope and love of Jesus himself which the Church has articulated into the theological vision of its traditional belief-system, It is round this evangelical emphasis that the whole institution of the Church needs consciously and deliberately to continuously re-centre and re-form itself (*ecclesia semper reformanda*).

But history, as we know, has an inevitably casual way of unfolding, and reformation and renewal are never more than partial at best, and are as time-bound as what they try to reform and renew. Given what we refer to as human nature, they are unlikely to be consistently or efficiently undertaken, and they are looked to chiefly to ward off some passing error, to correct some past over-emphasis or to satisfy some passing fashion. It is at such junctures that what can later look like distortions or omissions in the tradition can occur. The Catholic Church, if it were being consistently true to itself and less subject to the vagaries of history, should be possessed by a single, constant spiritual energy, with its material and institutional components wholly subservient to its radically evangelical purposes. That it plainly remains imperfect is the price that has to be paid for being, as Newman saw, 'a fact in the world's history', and for not yet having adapted itself as often or as profoundly as it should have done to its own founding inspiration.

Looked at in the plain light of day, the institutional Church is a socially established reality consisting almost entirely of lay men and women whose spiritual lives are serviced largely by a male clerical hierarchy who form a tiny minority of the whole body, which is meant to share responsibility for the promotion and continuing development of the Catholic tradition of faith and beliefs. The Church is Catholic in at least this sense – that it is meant to be comprehensively classless in its membership. If there is any means test that qualifies a person for membership, it consists in showing that you are human. No one who is a member of the Church can be more Catholic than anyone else. Is the Pope Catholic? – then equally so is the barefoot Andean peasant woman working her stony Incan terraces.

> For just as the body is one and has many members, and all the members of the body, though many, are one body, so it is with Christ. For in the one Spirit we were all baptized into one body – Jews or Greeks, slaves or free – and we were all made to drink of one Spirit. (1 Corinthians 12:12–13)

No amount or degree of the diversity in status or function within the institutional Church alters this basic, comprehensive truth. Diversity is one thing, inequality is quite another. In fact, the evangelical nature of the Church shows that it is specifically meant to counter our habitual evaluations of status and function by positively discriminating in favour of the underprivileged:

> On the contrary, the members of the body that seem to be weaker are indispensable, and those members of the body that we think less honourable we clothe with greater honour, and our less respectable members are treated with greater respect; whereas our more respectable members do not need this. (1 Corinthians 12:22–24)

But it is undeniable that the sense of obvious inequality among members of the Church which St Paul was trying to correct in the first-century Corinthian community still bedevils twenty-first-century Roman Catholicism.

It is, however, equally undeniable that Catholicism could not survive, let alone flourish, without some form of organized institution to establish and represent the presence of Catholicism as a religion in the world, and to monitor and promote the necessary development of its traditional system of beliefs and practices by which salvific faith is supported and deepened – matters which, as I have been suggesting, are essential to Catholicism as a particular religion in a real world. On the other hand, it also has to be admitted that the widespread authoritative power of the exclusively male and clerical minority establishment of the Church, run for so long from Rome, has meant that this minority establishment has acquired the ingrained habit of identifying the Church proper with itself, virtually reducing the bulk of the faithful majority to a species of hangers-on or camp-followers. Those in responsible roles in the institutional Church, whose reason for being in those roles is simply to serve the faithful majority and service their religious needs, have contrived to 'reify' themselves into the institution itself. This cannot be right, and it seems to me the most serious imbalance which threatens the well-being and effective functioning of the Church. From it there follow the other distortions which deface the Church as we know it – the by now scandalous refusal to grant full human equality in the functioning of the Church to women, the overbearing style in which authority and power are still used with little regard to truth, the reluctance to encourage laypeople to think and act like the mature adult Catholics they are supposed to be, and the exclusive mentality which still underlies preaching and practice not only towards other religions but also towards other Churches of the Christian persuasion.

These are heavy charges, and they have no doubt been well substantiated and discussed elsewhere. I note them simply in passing as seriously disabling, and still apparently permanent, obstacles to the way the Church is supposed to work out its evangelical mission, and hence to the wider spread of the salvific truth of Catholicism. I do not wish to go into further detail about what are, after all, predictable problems in any human institution where an acquisitive establishment has been led to appropriate the opportunity to exploit the rest. Nor is Catholicism the only religious system in which such problems occur. It has become commonplace to blame the world's religions for most of the world's destructive tensions; and on the face of it, the charge can be made to sound plausible. But a deeper look reveals, I think, that it is not so much the religions that are at fault as the way in which they have organized themselves as institutions and failed to fulfil their founding purposes. Three common factors are, to my mind, chiefly responsible. First, unbalanced centralization: that is, either too much religious authority and power are exercised from the centre – or, in some cases, too little. Second, male clericalization: that is, religious authority and power have become vested in a self-serving class of male professional clergy – a problem seriously aggravated, in my view, by the celibacy imposed in the Catholic system. Third – and in my judgement the most important disabling factor – chronically sub-standard and fundamentalistic theology: that is, a seriously impoverished and literal understanding of a religion's traditional scriptures and belief-system, despising intelligent interpretation, and rigorously imposed on a religion's followers to the point where the tradition no longer serves to support the distinctive faith-vision in which those followers are meant to share. In more or less subtle ways, these three factors are often interlinked – and not least the second and third. Matters are made worse when it is realized that, within Catholicism at least, it remains true that there are simply no sound theological, religious or spiritual reasons why such factors should be considered at all irreformable. However, I would count the kind of reforms I consider necessary in the institutional Catholic Church (even if I thought them possible) as pointless without some radical reappraisal of the whole religion and spirituality of Catholicism of the kind I have been trying to suggest. So I can leave criticism of the Church largely to others. Institutionally the Church presents a soft target, and in constantly attacking it, it is easy to lose sight of the formidable amount of good it has long contrived to do – and still does – in the world despite its manifest shortcomings. I like to think I have a more positive purpose.

What I think needs to be done is to relocate the institutional Church in a role – far less grandiose and far more evangelical – where, with its interior imbalances adjusted, it might fulfil the function that would be required of it in the kind of Catholicism I have been discussing. All my attempts at suggesting the reappraisal of Catholicism as a distinctly humane spirituality have advocated, not the destruction of the features which strictly belong to Catholicism as a religion, but a radical rebalancing of them – either the salvaging of neglected features in the tradition and their elevation to their proper prominence, or the relegation of hitherto over-prominent elements to their proper place. In this way it has become possible for primary elements like the humanity of Jesus and his human faith, along with an appreciation of the metaphorical nature of theology and the role the religious imagination plays in it, to be brought to the fore; whilst the Catholic system of doctrines and beliefs has been assigned its indefeasible function in giving intelligible expression to the religious vision of reality which the faith of Jesus and of Catholicism entail. In this necessary re-prioritization nothing need be lost, but some hitherto familiar features of Catholicism will need to be relegated; and one of them, I am sure, will be the power (as distinct from the quite proper religious and spiritual authority and leadership) of Rome, exercised as it often is to the detriment of the religious and spiritual authority which rightly belongs to more particular and local Catholic churches and communities; though in fairness to Rome it is right to add that local churches may sometimes be suspected of indulging a habit of subservience to Rome which is not justified by their canonical rights and status. It is as if an excessively ultramontane devotion to Rome were demanded as a proof of loyalty.

It is therefore important to determine the place and function of the institutional Church in the religion and spirituality of Catholicism. On a personal note: the Church has exercised a dominant influence over long stretches of my own life, and I am far from ungrateful for the personal benefits I derived from having been called on to play certain privileged roles in its service. But I found that the more I complied with the institutional Church's powerful imposition of its own heavily systematic and so often impersonal approach to what constituted religion and spirituality, the less sure I became that I was on the right road to that fully human salvation involved in coming to the right terms with the humanly grounded mystery Catholics call God – a way of salvation which, as I saw it, the religion and spirituality of Catholicism was supposed to offer. In the end, I thought, this salvation had to come to me from God, the mystery which defined my being human, through my sharing the faith-vision of Jesus in accepting the beliefs of Catholicism. Where Catholicism, in my view, promised that faith, hope and love shared with Jesus would vouchsafe transforming insights into the human condition and into its remarkable potential for an ever fuller, more open human life lived in an ordinary world imaginatively construed in terms of my Catholic beliefs, my long experience of the institutional Church had found that these life-enhancing effects had been kept locked up in crudely simplified and reach-me-down formulas and practices – had been, so to speak, predigested by the authorities to be spoon-fed back on appropriate occasions to a largely passive membership in reduced and suitably diluted form. The faithful were in danger of being spiritually sold short. The Church seemed intent on offering no more of Catholic truth than would fit into an impersonal system which would provide everyone with all they would need to carry them through this vale of tears into some supposed world beyond. The mystery and the potential for sharing divinity which is involved in being human were being, as it were, drained out of Catholicism. In effect, there was little room for religion and personal spirituality, since they were hardly needed, and might serve only as a distraction from the demands of the system. In my own case a certain disillusionment set in, and I found that I would have to look more deeply into the Church, below the surface of its usual workings, in an attempt to see where and how the life-enhancing and death-confronting approach to life, the personal holiness and wisdom, that characterized the faith of Jesus and Catholicism proper, might still be available. But I am sure that there is nothing in this criticism of the Church that has not already been better expressed elsewhere.

☙

In any case, the concept of 'the Church' is not all that straightforward. When Catholics declare in the creed that 'we believe in one, holy, catholic and apostolic Church', they are, according to the view of Catholic belief-statements I have adopted above, not referring directly to the institutional Church as we happen to know it. Not only is it difficult to see the religious point or purpose of declaring a belief in the obvious case of 'a fact in the world's history'; but even the most ardent Catholic would hardly suppose that the Church as we know it is complete in its unity, its holiness or its universality or indeed in its complete conformity with the inchoate religion of the apostolic community inspired by Jesus. Rather, when Catholics formally declare that they believe in 'the Church', they are employing a theological metaphor (transferring the meaning from other gatherings or assemblies) to give expression to what they rightly see as a key component in their faith-induced vision of reality – the ultimate gathering of humankind into the salvation offered by Jesus. In fact, it seems to me that the metaphor might first be found in the figuratively charged context in which Jesus himself solemnly declared: 'you are Peter, and on this rock I will build my church, and the gates of Hades will not prevail against it' (Matthew 16:18). In a text that has long been hijacked by the institutional Church as referring to itself, 'church' does not, of course, refer to a Church whose institutional reality in Rome Jesus somehow foresaw, but – if indeed the remark came from Jesus at all – it would much more plausibly refer to Jesus' imaginative way of speaking about his hopes for a united community of followers under the initial leadership of Simon Peter. It is in this metaphorical sense that Catholic belief in the Church appears in the earliest extant creeds (from the second century), and in the creeds still used today.

It has been a standing temptation for the institutional Church to claim as literally true of itself the grand theological metaphors which the body (another metaphor) of believers has created for itself in the course of its long history. But we are dealing with theologoumena, products of the theological imagination, which understand the world community of Catholic believers in terms of 'the people of God', the assembly (*ekklesia*), or 'church' of those who share the Spirit of Christ and constitute his 'Mystical Body' in which the wide variety of its members are 'incorporated' – these are more or less helpful efforts at the metaphorical understanding of the communal effect of participating in the salvation which Catholicism has to offer, although it would not be difficult to point out the limitations they share with many metaphors. They are not to be taken literally as descriptions of the actual, existing, institutional Church, which, at least from time to time, has been only too willing to claim, or suggest, that they are precisely that. They represent expressions of belief and call for careful understanding as ways in which the community of believers chooses to see itself within the vision of reality afforded by sharing the faith of Jesus. We have to beware of their being taken over as triumphalistically literal descriptions of the Catholic Church we know.

By taking over theological and metaphorical expressions and ascribing them literally to itself, the institutional Church long ago inaugurated a programme of self-aggrandizement which has led to its regarding itself as the actual object in which Catholics must formally declare they believe in their creed. It is this deeply entrenched attitude on the part of Rome, along with all the ceaseless propaganda that supports it, that urgently requires that the institutional Church, important though it is, be relegated to its own level of actual reality. The institutional and centralized Church has promoted itself, over the centuries, to the virtual status of an end-in-itself, whereas it cannot possibly be more than the means of preaching and practising the evangelically based religion and spirituality of Catholicism, and of promoting the salvation it exists to serve. It is the means whereby the religious and spiritual needs of those who share the Catholic religion which is grounded in the faith-vision of Jesus are served. The faithful are not there to be made subjects but to be guided and helped towards the salvation which their Cathoic religion offers. Salvation, the fulfilment of our humanity, I have maintained, consists in living with the vision of reality which Catholicism has to offer, a vision shared with Jesus and inspired by his faith, hope and love. Hence this is the absolute priority of the Church and the evangelical standard by which its performance should be judged – it must ensure that the salvific vision of reality is being made appropriately available to all its members, whatever their age, gender, education, cultural background, material situation and spiritual condition. Of course, it is all very grand and easy to pontificate in this way, as if the Church were nothing more than a large business venture which simply seemed to need a new 'Mission Statement' and some new corporate aims. We still need to be clearer about what we understand by 'the Church'.

※

Besides the Church in the institutional sense, it is possible to distinguish two other important senses in which 'the Catholic Church' may be understood – as universal, and more importantly, as sacramental.

'Catholic' means, of course, universal. Saying what the universality of the Catholic Church consists in requires some care. A particular institution among other religious institutions, it can claim to be universal only to the extent that the salvation it offers and for which it is responsible retains its universal validity – that is, to the extent that Catholic salvation remains open and applicable to the whole range of humanity. There is an element of paradox in play here. The Catholic Church is a particular and, in my view, a highly distinctive institution whose mission is universal, in the sense that the salvation it offers is the salvation of humanity precisely as such. It is the universality of its mission that earns the label Catholic, not the fact that the Church happens to consider itself a universally authoritative institution. It was once fashionable for theologians to seek to include all people of good will – 'anonymous Christians' or even sincere believers in other religions – in some limitlessly extended, almost ghostly version of the Catholic Church, and to claim that the Church's universality derived from the God-given authority it had over everybody. Not only must this unconvincing claim be judged intolerably arrogant in itself (why was it assumed that everyone should be happy to belong, in any sense, to the Catholic Church?), but also self-destructive in its effect, since it attenuates to the point of nonentity both the specific kind of religious faith and the profession of distinctive beliefs which belong to Catholicism. My point is that the Church's claim to be universal does not rest on anything that the institutional Church is or has achieved, but on the saving mission which it is supposed to be fulfilling. Its universality is grounded, not on any triumphalistic claim to universality, but on the universality of the human appeal of the religion and spirituality it is meant to represent. The Church is universal, in other words, because it promotes a faith, the faith of Jesus, which is ultimately a faith in the existential mystery which surrounds and determines the very essence of what we mean by being human. This saving mystery, as we have seen, comes to a particular, distinctive, but still universally relevant form of expression in Catholicism and its system of beliefs. It is the Church's evangelical task to ensure that its mission effectively promotes this universal Catholicism in a world of endlessly particular diversities.

But the question of how the institutional Church is meant to perform this task remains unanswered. For an answer we must turn, I think, to what is called the sacramentality of the Church – in other words, to the idea that the Church is meant to work, to achieve its spiritual effect, after the manner of a sacrament. So important do I think this idea to be, that I would count sacramental effectiveness as the second vital criterion of Catholicism. The concept of sacrament, it must be said, can have a broader application than that with which most people are familiar. The concept has been, as I shall explain below, usefully applied to Jesus as the incarnate Son of God. He might be intelligently understood as the sacrament of God – as the outward and visible sign of the inward and invisible mystery of God, a reality which he makes real and present in himself, and thus in the world of humankind, precisely in and through being the uniquely effective sign of it. But undoubtedly the seven sacraments are what Catholics know best. Sacraments are believed to work, to be effective, precisely through being signs. But it is not easy to adjust our minds to this specialized kind of spiritual causality, and we are always tempted to suppose that in the dispensation of the sacraments such reality as is believed to be enacted or made real – usually thought of as some form of grace – could or might occur or becomes real in some way independently of the sacramental process: that the sacraments are celebrated, as it were, just to provide a ritual occasion or setting for what 'really' takes place. It was for emptying the sacraments themselves of their content and efficacy that this Protestant view incurred the ultimate condemnation of the Council of Trent:

> If a person were to say that the sacraments of the New Law *do not contain the grace which they signify, or that they do not confer that grace itself to those who present no obstacle to it,* as if they were no more than signs of grace or justification received through faith, and some sort of mark [*notae quaedam*] of the Christian profession by which the faithful are distinguished from the infidel among men – let him/her be anathema.
> (Session VII, 3 March 1547, Denzinger-Schönmetzer, #1606, my translation and italics)

'Contain', 'confer' are words which unambiguously indicate that in Catholic thinking the earthly, ordinary, material factors which belong to the sacramental process – the words, the bread, the wine, the water, the oil, the hands imposed, the sexual union of marriage partners – themselves actually serve as the causally effective vehicles of that salvation which Catholicism has to offer, the salvation that consists, as I have been arguing, in that self-transcendence which involves sharing the faith, hope and love of Jesus in response to the demands of our common humanity, and sharing that vision of reality which the Catholic belief-system has elaborated on the basis of that basic faith, hope and love.

We might look at the sacraments in this way: through its seven sacraments Catholicism ensures that our share in the grace of that saving vision of reality is first imparted (baptism), then strengthened (confirmation), and later, in certain cases, directed to the active service of the community (orders). These three sacraments are non-repeatable because they are thought to impose their particular stamp (the 'character' of the sacrament) on a person for life. In the other sacraments the grace of the vision is boosted to counter the lowering effect of poor health and approaching death (the sacrament of the sick, once called extreme unction); or the vision is restored, when it has become blurred or obscured by sin and forgiveness is sought (the sacrament of reconciliation, or penance). In the remaining two sacraments that saving grace is constantly expanded and fortified by being shared in the permanent mutual love of a man and a woman in marriage (matrimony); and – to come to the crown of the whole sacramental system – the nourishment and enhancement of Jesus' saving vision, along with the whole sacrificial thrust of his life of faith, hope and love, comes through contact with Jesus himself in his sacramentally real presence in the consecrated bread and wine of the Eucharist, the sacrament celebrated at the Catholic Mass.

It is key to any understanding of Catholicism, visionary and mystical as I have suggested its origins and workings to be, that it is seen as remaining wholly grounded and embedded in, and effectively dependent on, the ordinary materiality of human life. Nothing, it might be said, can be of the same significance outside or beyond this sublunary world. If – as is certainly the case – the Church has succeeded in giving the impression that Catholicism really exists to deal chiefly with what supposedly lies beyond this world, that the salvation it offers consists in the final achievement of some other-worldly state which mirrors life in this world, then that impression must be severely countered by the fact that the Catholic salvation for which the Church is responsible relates to and affects people in their current, down-to-earth lives. It is precisely to effect this that Catholicism needs to be mystical and visionary in the ways I have tried to suggest. I have hinted earlier that I am not too sure whether Catholicism should be simply classified as a religion, since it deals with the spiritual in ways that are so distinctively different from other religions as to make such a classification at least potentially misleading. As a spirituality, Catholicism seems to me to be at once profoundly mystical and at the same time utterly prosaic. It is because of this that I have preferred to deal with Catholicism in radically humanistic terms. As I see it, what we have in Catholicism might be briefly and best described as a thorough materialization of the spiritual which effects the proper spiritualization of the material. The Church may try to be unworldly, to distance itself from the world by being other-worldly; but other-worldliness can be escapist and thoroughly misleading – just an easy way out of the central, thoroughly worldly task for Catholicism which is the construction, and reconstruction, of a here-and-now human world in which our defective humanity is firmly countered and raised from the deadness towards which it is biased. It is the sacramental counter-worldliness of Catholicism which, far from being in any way escapist, should constitute that distinctive, universally applicable, humanly effective, spiritual worldliness – or worldly spirituality – which it exists to foster. It seems to me that it is against this as a criterion that the institutional Church's performance of its salvific mission may be most properly judged.

Reflections such as these take their rise from a quality which is so pervasive in Catholicism that it has been called 'the principle of sacramentality', seen as basic to an understanding of Catholicism and its workings. 'Sacramentality' is a technical theological expression which serves as a general description of Catholicism's distinctive emphasis on the causal involvement of material factors in its approach to the spiritual. As I have already mentioned, it is possible, and enlightening, to speak of Christ as the sacrament of the Catholic God, in virtue of his being the embodiment or incarnation of what is meant by God in Catholicism – 'for in him the whole fullness of deity dwells bodily ...' (Colossians 2:9). It is, sacramentally speaking, the material, bodily reality of Jesus which is the effective sign of God, in that it is the historical, human Jesus, born of Mary and who died on the Cross, who renders God real and active among us. For Catholicism, obviously, Jesus himself exemplifies the supreme instance of the principle of sacramentality in operation.

Can something analogous be usefully said about the institutional Church as a whole? After all, it maintains a considerable material presence and activity throughout much of the inhabited world, and its mission is to bring a distinctive form of spiritual salvation to all. So given the supreme example of the incarnation itself, it does not seem to me unreasonable, following the general principle of sacramentality, to try, *mutatis mutandis*, to understand the institutional Church in terms of a working sacrament of Catholic salvation, and to judge its performance in terms of its sacramental effectiveness. The advantage of this approach, so it seems to me, is that it is at least a religiously principled approach to criticism of the institutional Church, in a field where criticism is, more often than not, based on prejudice, on party interests, on anecdote and, perhaps most of all, on ignorance. So the questions may be posed: does the institutional Church fulfil its mission in a way that is consonant with its sacramental nature? Is it sacramentally effective in preserving and propagating the salvation it is meant to represent? Does its whole materiality – its centralized and hierarchical organization, its wealth, its style and tone, its leadership, its liturgies, its teachings, its outreach to all nations, its local presence – do all these, and other, material factors serve, after the manner of a sacrament, to make real and available to all people the sort of spiritual salvation that, as I have been suggesting, consists in a person's sharing in that vision of reality which is entailed by sharing the faith, hope and love of Jesus?

So how well does the institutional Church function sacramentally? Does the Church as an institution succeed in making real for people the spiritual salvation of whose presence and efficacy it is the material sign? Once again, I do not think that there is a simple answer to such questions. In many respects no doubt the Church functions at least satisfactorily as a sacrament, and its active presence in the world continues to make available and to bring about the salvation of which it is the visible sign. To the jaded and disillusioned Western world this may seem an exaggerated claim to make; but it would be easy to defend it with regard, let us say, to the more deprived parts of Africa or South America – even from my own brief and superficial observations in Zimbabwe and Peru. And it must be remembered, of course, that if the Church had not been functioning with some measure of sacramental effectiveness in the past, we would not be here to raise questions about it.

I am strongly inclined to think that whilst there is much that is right about the sacramental functioning of the Church, its effect is flawed by three kinds of failure: in the first place – a point on which I have already touched – doctrinally speaking, the Church has recently given the impression of lacking the courage of its own convictions when it comes to teaching all its members clear knowledge and understanding of the doctrines that make up its creed – the authoritative theologoumena which I have described as articulating the faith-vision in which salvation consists. For one thing, the Church still persists in looking on its traditional doctrines as a closed system of truths and certitudes in which to train its clergy so that, without crucial questions of meaning being raised, it can be imposed as a take-it-or-leave-it system on a passive laity. But whilst it may be currently unfashionable to insist on clear knowledge of traditional doctrines, compliance with this trend may well contribute substantially to failure in the sacramental efficacy of the Church's work. This is because Catholicism offers a saving faith-vision, in the organic structuration and articulation of which the Church's traditional doctrines play a crucial part. So it remains a key part of the Church's sacramental function to ensure that the saving faith of Catholicism is effectively imparted in all its doctrinal and credal orthodoxy. Orthodoxy cannot be simply understood as the theological correctness for its own sake demanded by a fussy or interfering Church authority. Orthodoxy is organic to the whole Catholic spirituality. It is a matter of ensuring that the proper saving vision is effectively preserved, maintained and sacramentally passed on. Perhaps this hesitancy of the Church over doctrine receives some confirmation from the failure of

Vatican II to temper papal infallibility (and with it the dominance of Rome) by firmly defining the infallibility of the Church in terms of the collegial authority of the Church's bishops. I recall that many responsible bishops and their theologians knew at the time that this was exactly what needed doing at the Council, but nothing doctrinally effective was in fact done.

A second kind of failure which undermines that sacramental effect of the Church's work is the intransigence which the Church establishment occasionally manifests towards certain issues which are religiously neutral in themselves, and which, if they were imaginatively tackled, could greatly increase the Church's sacramental efficacy. An obvious example of such an issue would be the introduction of married men and women priests. It is impossible to imagine what loss there would be of sacramental effect if priests, men and women, were married and had families. Many might think that the sacramental effect would be much increased. It is arbitrarily pointless, and a sign of weakness, to exclude even the discussion of such an issue. In fact, of course, married men priests operate effectively in some places already. But clearly by far the worst example of institutional intransigence is the arbitrary exclusion of women, married and unmarried – at least half the human race – from the ordained ministry of the Church. It is not possible to frame any sound argument – theological, organizational, social, and least of all religious and spiritual – in support of this ban whereby the human sacramental resources of the Church remain so severely curtailed. Care, however, needs to be taken in reassessing the whole role of the clergy in the Church before simply deciding to boost their numbers. Merely quantitative solutions are not what are needed. The aim in all the Church's doings should be to conform to the evangelical and sacramental criteria.

A third kind of failure is more difficult to define since it has, in my view, less to do with obvious issues than with the overall style or tone of the male clerical establishment which is directly responsible for the Church's mission. Nonetheless, it remains true that sacramental efficacy can be seriously impaired by the adoption of the wrong manner and the wrong approach. I happen to think that in many of the issues – and not least the personal and sexual issues – that are commonly debated nowadays the views of the Church are both sensible and generally right. The Church's views may not be the only possible views, but there can be no doubt that they have enjoyed the benefit of long maturation and considerable experience. That they are currently unfashionable may be unfortunate. But the virtually automatic rejection of those views by contemporary society has a great deal to do, not with the views themselves – which, far from being expressions of religious fanaticism, tend to be based on ordinary and unexciting common sense – but with the manner and tone which the Church's establishment adopts in expecting compliance with them. The wrong manner and the wrong tone can certainly spoil the sacramental quality and efficacy of the Church's leadership.

It may seem trivial to charge the Church's establishment with failing to adopt the right manner and the right tone. But no Catholic needs to live and work in Rome to experience what might be globally called the Roman style of Church governance. It silently permeates the institutional Church from the highest level down to the local parish. Catholics have become so accustomed to it that many notice its effects only rarely. Some think they would be lost without it, and wonder how other Churches survive in its absence. Others strongly resent it and make other arrangements. This Roman style has to do, above all, with the vigorous exercise of centralized power and is, among the hierarchy and with a certain kind of male celibate clergy, highly contagious. The style is broadly authoritarian, claiming the right to be obeyed without demur. Non-compliance is threatened with punishment, if only in some next world. The chief purpose of the exercise of authoritative power seems to be to put the non-compliant in bad faith. The Church comes across as totalitarian in the sense that its members are subjected to an all-or-nothing regime. It is intent on keeping the real exercise of power in the hands of a centralized coterie. Of course it is possible to interpret this practice as a means of ensuring the overall pastoral good of the faithful, as good shepherding; no doubt this worthy aim is what those in authority think they have in mind. But it does not need to be emphasized how this style of governance can often render the sacramental effect of the work of the institutional Church null and void. Whatever else, it is not the right style of the twenty-first century, nor indeed for any century which followed the life and death of the inspirer of Catholicism.

I should add that I have been privileged to have some brief and superficial personal experience of ecclesiastical life in the Roman corridors of power, and I have been struck by the extent to which the Church's shortcomings are embedded in the institutional system which has been adopted over the centuries. It often seemed to me that most of the system's operators were notably human in their ways, but that they could not imagine how the Roman system of governance might be open to change. It was what they had inherited, and they had become its victims. Perhaps it was this which led them to make victims of others.

The Church is sacramental in the sense that it is meant to signal and produce the effective presence of the reality it stands for – the salvation offered to humankind in the acceptance of the faith-vision of Jesus. What I am suggesting is that this function would be better performed if the Church attended to the development and maintenance of the saving vision through its doctrines, its traditional system of beliefs, its worship, its preaching and its liturgy; if the Church was open to the frank discussion of contemporary issues which should include not only relatively easy internal arrangements like the introduction of married clergy and women priests and bishops, but should also embrace far more difficult external matters such as war, poverty, economic imperialism, arms-dealing, and so forth. No doubt there are many in the Church who impress by their active engagement with such issues; but they are not usually those who are supposed to be the Church's leaders. It is for the Church's leaders to adopt a style and manner of governance which let the faithful play their rightful, sacramentally imparted role in the Church's sacramental work. At its centre the Church seems sacramentally blunt, obtuse, out of touch and out of date. The effects of the great 'work worked' by Jesus, the *opus operatum*, done 'for us and for our salvation', do not get as effectively imparted to the world as they should be. The Church's only important reason for existing is to impart these effects which flow 'from the work worked' once and for all – *ex opere operato*; and the higher the Church's overall sacramental quality, the more effectively it fulfils its mission.

Of course, all I have so roughly said still requires careful formulation and much discussion; but all I have done is to apply to the Church as a whole those precepts which the Church itself laid down at Vatican II for 'the appropriate renewal of religious life' in its own religious communities. Renewal is said to involve two simultaneous processes:

1. a continuous return to the sources of all Christian life and to the original inspiration behind a given community and
2. an adjustment of the community to the changed conditions of the times (*Perfectae Caritatis*, 2).

No amount of ecclesiastical tinkering or the trivializing of vital issues will any longer serve the increasingly urgent questions which the Church has still to face, both within and without, if it is to fulfil its sacramental task effectively. A radical reappraisal of the Catholicism for which it is responsible would, I am convinced, need to be completed first. Many in the world want a truly spiritual religion, and, in my view, Catholicism, with all its potential as a universal human spirituality, is, were it to operate in accordance with the evangelical and sacramental criteria that apply to it, best placed to provide it through a Church which actually met those criteria.

Conclusion

I had reservations from the start about the likelihood of discovering that 'final belief' in Catholicism which seemed so desirable a way of imposing closure on the questions that had been raised in the course of my long experience of the Catholic religion, its spirituality, its theology, its practices, its discipline and its churchmanship. But I had decided to try to revisit what had become so familiar in the hope of discovering an approach to understanding it all which would not only take account of its complexity, but also interpret it in such a way as give it all a simpler, more coherent, spiritual sense which would render it more credible. I wanted to find the working spirituality behind all that I already knew of Catholicism. There was, of course, a certain artificiality about this procedure. I felt like a person who had been brought up in a stately home, who had lived there for a good long time, who had never really left it for anywhere else, and who was now revisiting the place as an informed visitor, out to view his old home with a new and more critical eye from a different angle. Becoming a visitor in an already deeply familiar place proved difficult. All the same, the visit has proved helpful. Perhaps the most important lesson I have learned is that Wallace Stevens' initial challenge has proved, at least as far as my native Catholicism is concerned, stimulating but empty.

In the first place, it is clear that the prologues are not over – that they will stop only with death. Try as I might to formulate for myself some satisfyingly definitive understanding of Catholicism, I have not really done so. My understanding has increased, but it is quirky, idiosyncratic, over-subjective. I may be on the right lines in the matter of 're-imagining God', but I do not feel I have advanced far down them. I think, however, that I have moved closer to the heart of Catholicism; and I have realized that I shall have to go on asking questions – and perhaps better questions – about it. My understanding of it all is deeper and more human that it ever was before, and it seems better suited to providing a basis for a personal spirituality than anything I learned about Catholicism previously. But the prologues are not over. The spiritual life to which Catholicism is an invitation is a life of ongoing personal growth, of the further knowledge and appropriation of our personal mystery (or God), a life which aims at a continuous healing and enrichment of the self through the self-transcendence which is to be found in the faith, hope and love which enable us to respond to the demands which belong to our humanity – the faith, hope and love which we draw from the Spirit of the crucified and risen Jesus. In this process there is clearly still room for more prologues to come.

Secondly, given the open-endedness of the process of the personal spiritual growth which Catholicism is meant to promote, there can be no question of 'final belief'. The reason for this, as I have tried to explain, is that Catholic belief – the traditional belief-system – and the changing understanding of it required by the process of personal maturation from what St Paul saw as religious infancy to spiritual adulthood will therefore always remain open to further development. Or as Wittgenstein realized, unless a person is prepared to mature religiously and spiritually, the beliefs of the Catholic system can only continue to be in some measure misunderstood. The way in which the Catholic belief-system is understood – the meaning it has for us – plays an integral role in the depiction of the spiritual vision which faith, hope and love have of the reality of the world. To allow that vision to continue to deepen and grow, the belief-system which structures it into an intelligible vision must remain open to further interpretation and understanding. The process must not be foreclosed by treating Catholic beliefs as if their meaning can be grasped in its fullness once and for all, as if faith were meant to terminate in an unthinking certainty, and as if certainty were the most desirable quality of faith. To treat Catholic beliefs in this way would be to stunt the faith, hope and love which depend on them for their fuller expression.

Thirdly, although there appears to be every reason for understanding Catholic beliefs, and indeed all theological language, metaphorically, this is not the same as declaring that they amount to no more than a fiction. Insofar as they are human linguistic artefacts and constructions, theological beliefs must have their origins in the processes of human creativity. They depend on the interpretative activity of the human imagination as a way of understanding – of coming to terms with – what cannot be otherwise expressed and understood; whereas the method and purpose of fiction, in its common meaning, lies in invention. As a truth-telling literary technique, fiction works through invention, even though it will maintain its reference to the world. But the point is that the world to which fiction relates, quite unlike the world or vision expressed by theological beliefs, is a world that might be expressed otherwise. It could be straightforwardly described, analysed, measured, grasped by the senses; and most fiction presents its world as such. This is precisely what theological beliefs cannot be expected to do. They can work only indirectly, 'slant', obliquely, metaphorically, employing such linguistic resources as come usefully to hand to get across what they want to say. If theology is fiction, then it is – to parody what C. S. Lewis said of theology as poetry – very bad fiction. Theological beliefs, rather, are figurative attempts to present a picture of the vision of reality which inspires persons for whom the faith, hope and love of Jesus are the mainsprings of their daily lives.

Fourthly, I think it is misleading to suggest that, in the end, holding Catholic beliefs or not is simply a matter of choice that 'it is time to choose'. Of course, a person may feel free to hold them or reject them. I myself feel free to do either, but I do not feel that I have a choice in the matter. Being free and having a choice, at least in serious matters which touch on the core of being human, seem to be not at all the same thing. We can hardly be said to have a choice whether we wish to be human or to become more human, or not, however free we may feel about it. In fact, it might even be said that the less choice we have in the matter, the more free we feel we are to become more fully human. Choosing to deny our humanity – something we are all only too capable of doing in countless ways – is not something we have the freedom to do, as our rational consciences are only too quick to tell us. In fact it seems that the deliberate choice of any evil, far from being an exercise of our human freedom, points only to an enduring lack of it. I have suggested that the meaning of the Catholic belief-system lies in its use to provide an imaginative theological setting in which Catholics can meaningfully live their ordinary lives in pursuit of the spiritual values which will make those lives more fully human – lives, in other words, which are becoming self-transcendently more human as they respond with faith, hope and love to the demands of their mystery-laden, God-defined humanity. The trivializing notion that there comes a time to make a final, definitive choice which brings closure to the way we hold beliefs and uphold values that make us more human strikes me as an illusion. It is related to the corrosive illusion of certainty in spiritual matters. It is our daily human lot to have to go on searching out ways of deepening our faith, hope and love – of understanding our world better, of being less dominated by death and by the deadness within, and of letting our moral goodness develop under the influence of love. It is this basic human search that Catholicism exists to promote.

⚜

I can now see that I am going to have to live, not with doubts about Catholicism as a spiritual religion, but, whether I like it or not, with a continuing will to understand its meaning and its workings more deeply. There are two reasons for this: the first reason I have just given – the consolations of definitive certainty about the meaning and the workings of a Catholic spirituality which promotes the development of humanity as such are not available because humanity – or at least my humanity – is not a fixed item but a potential, if damaged and needy, source of permanent spiritual growth. There is no foreseeable limit to the extent to which – given the proper spiritual help (or grace), and provided I am willing to cooperate – my humanity might continue to transcend itself through faith, hope and love. The second reason is that, in the end, attempts to express the findings of my search must always resolve themselves in paradox – the paradox that I become more my real self by spiritually conforming to the Spirit-driven humanity I discern in Jesus. One of the uses of paradox is to signal the presence of inconclusiveness, a reasoned inability to impose closure on matters that by their very nature resist it. But here I find myself involved not in paradox in the strong sense of any logical self-contradiction, nor in paradox in the weak sense of what happens to run contrary to received or conventional opinion; but in the kind of technical or theological paradox which is the best we can hope to do by way of expressing the existential mystery that besets our being human, the mystery we call God. This was the mystery which Jesus came to discern in and through his own humanity – the difference from ourselves being that in his unique case the paradox was different. As his followers eventually came to express the matter theologically, he was believed to share personally in the very mystery that surrounds all humanity, possessed as he was of the perfect Spirit of Sonship of the Father. Nonetheless, his human life and death, it was believed, served to bring – 'for our sake and for our salvation – his innocent humanity, in terms of time and space and in a costly fashion, into conformity with that surrounding mystery. Where paradoxes such as these abide, there will always be a felt need to explore and refine its terms further. So 'final belief' turns out to be itself 'a fiction' – a figment, a phantom perhaps worth pursuing for a while, but not for ever.

I have maintained that the revelation on which Catholicism ultimately rests is a unique insight achieved by Jesus into what it is to be human. He re-imagined what was meant by being human, and thereby – in a theological paradox – he was led to re-imagine what it meant by God. Humanity and God were effectively re-pictured in terms of their newly revealed relationship. It is this new insight which requires a constant search for the best available way of understanding the new revelation of God and humanity. The new understanding cannot be achieved in terms that derive directly from systems of thought, either philosophical or religious, which were never designed to accommodate the new revelation. Yet existing terms have to be used – otherwise the new revelation could not be understood – but they have to drop their old meanings and be used with a new, spiritual meaning to make the best of the new expression required. The shift involves a conscious move to a less literal form of understanding – in fact, to the kind of spiritual understanding which St Paul wished to find in his converts. In understanding our own humanity in the revealing light of Jesus' own approach to being human, we come to understand it more spiritually – more in terms of its potential self-transcendence, a potential that needs to be activated through the human faith, hope and love which inspired Jesus. Having re-imagined our humanity on these new lines, we need to re-imagine our whole idea of the God who is our humanity's salvation. It is with this task that Catholic theologians have, in their timid way, busied themselves for centuries.

Not that they have been wholly unsuccessful: suitable theologoumena – scriptures, creeds, conciliar definitions and the like – have been produced in order to preserve the tradition of the crucial insight, and to keep alive the eventual possibility of further and deeper understandings of it. This might count as success enough in the troubled circumstances of history. But Catholic theology seems never to have developed its own spirit of adventure in searching out the spiritual depths of its own system. Perhaps theology was hijacked early on by an authoritarian Church and made to serve chiefly ecclesiastical interests, and not least the maintenance of power and control by a powerful clerical minority with mistaken pastoral concerns. But far more importantly, it seems to me, Catholic theology has been its own worst enemy. It has failed to note that its interpretative task cannot – because of the very nature of that task – be reduced and confined to the humdrum limits of human reason. Theology requires, above all else, the conscious boosting of the reason by the religious and spiritual imagination. Whilst a certain imaginative boosting cannot have been lacking – otherwise we would have had no theology at all – the active and conscious role of the imagination in theology (let alone in faith) has rarely, if ever, been acknowledged or exploited. Theology has preferred to adopt its worldly pose as a science, to enjoy academic respectability, to peddle what it likes to think of as its own rationalizing certainties. Because this attitude has suited the purposes of the institutional Church, theology has always received strong support from it. Meanwhile the crucial Catholic insight into humanity and the required radical shift in the re-imagined ideas both of God and of the relationship between man and God ran the risk of being lost, or at least of never really being understood in the spiritual terms of the Catholic faith-vision. The mystical quality of that vision and the mystery of God as it must now be imaginatively viewed from the depths of our own humanity were slipping through the coarse net of rationalistic understanding. Such, I think, are the reasons why I found it necessary to try, at least, to re-imagine and re-interpret Catholicism and to search for a better, more spiritual understanding of it.

I shall spell out, one last time, what I consider to be the foundational revelation with which Catholicism is meant to cope religiously, and of which it is meant to offer a spiritual understanding. To serious reflection humanity is revealed as being involved, existentially and essentially, in mystery – a defining condition which calls for an approach to it, and an outlook based on it, which can only be, strictly speaking, mystical. In terms of theological paradox, this amounts to saying that – mystically – in order to become its true self, to achieve its own full potential, being human calls for more than it can itself possibly provide by way of correction and support. In other words, there is always meant to be something more to humanity than what humanity itself can possibly offer. There must be self-transcendence. This inescapable 'more' of human self-transcendence is what, in the light of the above revelation, is what we must now re-imagine God – or in Jesus' characteristic parlance, 'the Father' – to be (*Deus semper maior*). We need to re-imagine God, not in second-hand, reach-me-down philosophical terms, but in terms of God being the mystery towards which our humanity has constantly to look for its meaning and its salvation. Without this newly conceived God, humanity runs the risk of risk of never fulfilling its potential, of being chronically deficient, of being what is theologically called sinful, of being still in need of being saved.

This unique and spiritual insight first dawned on Jesus out of the experience of his own humanity; and it was inherited as original and new from him by a handful of his followers. The insight called for a new and original expression which was appropriate, imaginatively intelligible and transmissible. From the start, this demand instantly put language under an unprecedented strain. Already stretching to cope with the semantic demands of existing religious ideas, the old linguistic wineskins needed to give way to fresh ones: 'Neither is new wine put into old wineskins; otherwise the skins burst, and the wine is spilled, and the skins are destroyed; but new wine is put into fresh wineskins, and so both are preserved' (Matthew 9:17). It was Catholic theology's task to provide fresh wineskins – a task, as I have said, which it may have performed well enough. In fact some might say that it has performed the task all too well, in that the fresh wineskins may well have preserved the new wine of Jesus' insight so carefully that few, so far, have had access to it; and most Catholics have had to rest content that the Church has it all safely bottled up and laid down for some future use.

From the start it became clear that a new religious world which was to be understood spiritually was what was being proposed. It is this fact that demands close attention to the meaning of words. My approach to Catholicism has reflected this necessity. It is not that I have an interest in indulging a fad for a certain kind of philosophy; but I feel sure that no one who takes the time to think seriously about the use of words in Catholic theology can remain unaware that, if the words used are to have any meaning, that meaning cannot be literal but (broadly speaking) metaphorical. Words whose meanings have always to be transferred from elsewhere are called for because Catholicism has to do, above all, with answering the question of how to become human; and according to its foundational insight into the matter, the very business of becoming human involves a mystical outlook, a vision of reality which owes nothing directly to the time and space matrix of our sublunary world, an attitude of faith, hope and love that cannot be reduced to a system of literal or scientific truths without being destroyed in the process. In the Catholic view, becoming human calls for our being taken spiritually out of ourselves if – paradoxically – we are ever to become ourselves, to be saved. This is the Catholic position with which its theological words have to cope. They must maintain the openness of our humanity that looks beyond what seems to be its native range. They must express what must remain outside the grasp of any understanding of humanity that might be offered by literal or scientific systems. Catholicism is grounded on a revelation of humanity which makes it clear that it lacks the means of achieving the spiritual fulfilment which it both needs and wants. Its chronic lack is supplied only by its mystical participation in the basic human virtues of faith, hope and love as these are discerned in the life, death and resurrection of Jesus. These are the virtues which ensure that humanity can meet the demands of its own basic necessities, and thus become itself. They are, for Catholicism, the defining human virtues (ineptly called 'theological') which constitute our mystical response to the God who is none other than the very mystery that surrounds our being the individual human persons we experience ourselves to be. They are the personal virtues which take us out of ourselves and thereby – paradoxically – constitute our only salvation.

These virtues are also the operative element in Catholicism as spiritually understood, as a spirituality. They work with an eye on the vision of reality which is vividly pictured in the theologoumena of the Catholic belief-system. Not that the vision works as an invitation to Catholics to withdraw from the common world and go and practice the saving virtues of faith, hope and love elsewhere – though the institutional Church, in its practical wisdom, has long provided various forms of spiritual refuge where the common spiritual life can be practiced by those who feel called to use those forms. But the common, Catholic spiritual life is meant to be led at the humdrum, quotidian, prosaic, commonplace level of completely human ordinariness – wherever, in fact, our humanity is called on to reveal itself in its true spiritual colours of faith, hope and love. For a few this may perhaps be at the altar or in the cloister, but it can also, with perfectly equal validity, be at the office desk or at the kitchen sink. Thus Catholicism is intensely this-worldly in a radical sense which may not true of other religions; and great care needs to be taken that the ornate trappings of institutional religion which Catholicism has acquired over the centuries do not distract from, or blunt, or impede, its essential thrust towards the salvation of the human, or obscure its shedding 'the true light that enlightens everyone coming into the world' (John 1:9 variant). So in Catholicism I find a radically mystical spirituality unremittingly focused, through faith, hope and love, on the salvation of the completely ordinary.

Notably paradoxical in the understanding of Catholicism and its workings is the fact that its downright spiritual emphasis on the completely ordinary level of human living employs such imaginatively vivid theologoumenal constructions as are to be found in its belief-system. But both sides of the paradox need to be maintained, because both work closely together, theology giving the necessarily imaginative backing to the down-to-earth spiritual practice of the virtues. Paradoxically, it takes theological metaphor to bring us to the full appreciation of the factual. It takes talk of the Beyond to express the deeper value of the Here-and-Now. It is precisely a paradox such as this that confronts us in Catholicism's central doctrine of the Incarnation. In the orthodox understanding of this doctrine, there is nothing of the fully divine which is not seen to be completely expressed in the ordinary, this-worldly, uniquely sinless human being called Jesus. Fully man, he is fully divine – he is in possession of everything that belongs to that mystery which surrounds our humanity and which we find it best to call God. He is everything we need, or can possibly want, to mean by God. When we call on him as God, we mean that in his unique humanity lies our salvation – a salvation we can best imagine overall in that other prime theologoumenon of Catholicism, the doctrine of the divine Trinity, since it is wholly in the Spirit of his utterly Son-like humanity that we are enabled to approach the mystery which we discern as Fathering us in our earth-bound individualities, and, through our mystical union with his Son's humanity, saving us from our sins. It is on these lines that Catholicism requires us to re-imagine radically what we mean by God.

There are many other possible paradoxical conclusions to be drawn about Catholicism understood as the spiritual religion it is meant to be. Universal in its scope, it has an intensely individual focus. Basically mystical in its origins, its functional application is primarily to completely ordinary human life. Highly institutionalized, its mission remains entirely personal and spiritual. Ornately structured, its programme of human salvation could hardly be simpler. Theologically sophisticated on the grandest of scales, its essential message could not be more down to earth. Deeply traditional, its spiritual meaning remains thoroughly contemporary. Rooted in the past, its only real interest is in the true future of mankind. Visionary as it is, it has nothing in its sights but the salvation of individual human beings. Such are the lessons that a spiritual understanding of Catholicism can teach. I was once led to think that it was all firmly based on some rational form of apologetics and on philosophical arguments. I have found that it makes spiritual sense only if it is seen to be based on the human mystery revealed in Jesus, and if it confronts, through all its elaborate developments, the difficulties of becoming human with its steady mystical stance.

So my search for the spiritual understanding of Catholicism has not, I think, been in vain. I have no doubt there are always deeper insights to come – insights to be achieved not through yet more dry and clumsy reflections on the meaning of Catholicism, but through the ordinary, daily, costly exercise of those virtues – faith, hope, love – which, as I have tried to show, form the heart of Catholicism's earth-bound spirituality. So, to return to St Paul: 'And now faith, hope and love abide, these three; and the greatest of these is love' (1 Corinthians 13:13) – all three so endlessly demanding, and love the most demanding but enduring of them all. But then as Philip Larkin observed: 'What will survive of us is love'. If so, then, as Louis Aragon remarked: 'Love is your last chance, there is nothing else to keep you here'. But perhaps it is William Wordsworth, arch-romantic as he was, who best captures how I would want to express the down-to-earth result of what I set out to discover:

> Enough, if something from our hands have power
> To live, and act, and serve the future hour;
> And if, as toward the silent tomb we go,
> Through love, through hope, and faith's transcendent dower,
> We feel that we are greater than we know.
> *(Valedictory Sonnet to the River Duddon)*

It is this practical ordinariness and this definitively human feeling that Catholicism, spiritually understood, exists to evoke, to promote, to enhance, to support, and to fulfil.

www.ingramcontent.com/pod-product-compliance
Lightning Source LLC
Chambersburg PA
CBHW071715160426
43195CB00012B/1683